52 more weeks of Dishcloths

A Knit Picks Kitchen Spectacular

Copyright 2016 © Knit Picks

All rights reserved. This book or any portion thereof may not be reproduced or used in any manner whatsoever without the express written permission of the publisher except for the use of brief quotations in a book review.

Photography by Amy Cave

Printed in the United States of America

Third Printing, 2017

ISBN 978-1-62767-113-2

Versa Press, Inc
800-447-7829

www.versapress.com

CONTENTS

January	**4**	Taj	76
Ice Crystal Face Cloth	6	Checks and Eyelets	80
Angor Wat	8	Happy Sheep	82
Market Day	10	Campfire	84
Snowbobbles	12	**August**	**86**
Diagonal	14	Beloeil	88
February	**16**	Brick-a-Brack	90
Field of Flowers	18	Pumpking	92
Tropical Vacation	20	Belted Stripes	94
Maritime Face Cloth	22	**September**	**96**
Queen of Hearts	24	Celebration	98
March	**26**	Ripples	100
King Charles	28	Slipped Stitches	102
Lydia's Lily Pad	30	Nice-n-Easy	104
Log Cabin	32	**October**	**106**
Granny's Rainbow	34	Radio Wave	108
April	**36**	Muiderslot	110
Petticoat	38	Summer Lines	112
Aztec	40	Ace of Spades	114
Sherbet Stripes	42	Big Zig	118
Bung Gudneau	44	**November**	**122**
Bicolor Tweed	46	Sunny Days	124
May	**48**	Heirloom Linen	126
Cabled Spa Cloth	50	Topaz Face Cloth	130
Something Blue	52	Black Diamond	132
Zig Zag	56	House of Clubs	134
Fishbones	58	**December**	**136**
June	**60**	Seaweed	138
Pinwheel	62	Tree Hunting	140
Caerphilly	64	Glacial Spa Cloth	142
Simple Lines	66	Vadstena	144
Square Check	68	Snowbank Spa Cloth	146
July	**70**	Meet the Designers	148
Love Music	72		

JANUARY

ICE CRYSTAL FACE CLOTH

by Joyce Fassbender

This face cloth is an ode to chilly winter weather with beautiful stranded colorwork. Fully charted, it features a stockinette colorwork center surrounded by a solid garter stitch border.

FINISHED MEASUREMENTS
9.5" wide x 11" high

YARN
Knit Picks CotLin (70% Tanguis Cotton, 30% Linen; 123 yards/50g): Main color: Swan 24134; Contrast color: Hydrangea 25772, 1 ball each.

NEEDLES
US 6 (4.0mm) straight or circular needles, or size to obtain gauge

NOTIONS
Yarn Needle

GAUGE
22 sts and 26 rows = 4" stockinette stitch

DIRECTIONS
CO 51 stitches using long tail cast on using main color (MC).

Knit five rows in main color.

Work Chart
Odd rows: k5 MC, k sts as indicated on chart, k5 MC.
Even rows: k5 MC, p sts as indicated on chart, k5 MC.

After completing chart, knit five rows in main color.

Finishing
Weave in ends, wash and block to size.

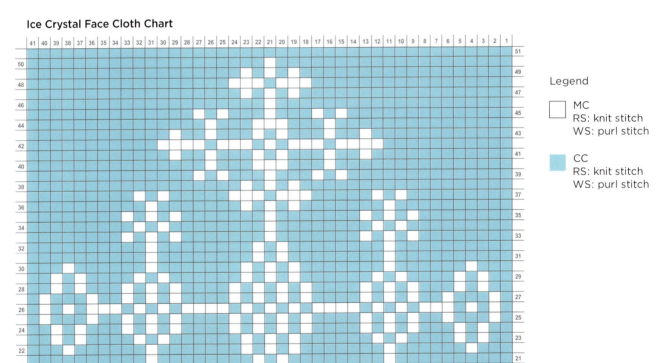

Ice Crystal Face Cloth Chart

Legend

MC
RS: knit stitch
WS: purl stitch

CC
RS: knit stitch
WS: purl stitch

ANGOR WAT

by Allyson Dykhuizen

Angkor Wat is a moated temple in Cambodia. Which has absolutely nothing to do with a dishcloth, except for the fact that it's a very beautiful set of buildings surrounded by water, much like this dishcloth is a pretty stitch pattern surrounded by applied i-cord. The body of the dishcloth is worked corner to corner in seed stitch, then stitches are picked up for an applied i-cord "moat", which will cover up any imperfections in your seed stitch edge and make it easy to add a loop for hanging.

FINISHED MEASUREMENTS
8.5" square, 1.25" hanging loop.

YARN
Knit Picks CotLin (70% Tanguis Cotton, 30% Linen; 123 yards/50g): Crème Brulee (MC) 24137, Coffee (CC) 24138, 1 ball each.

NEEDLES
US 5 (3.75mm) 16" circular and 2 DPNs, or size to obtain gauge

NOTIONS
Yarn Needle

GAUGE
20 sts and 32 rows = 4" in Seed Stitch, blocked.

Notes:

Seed Stitch (worked flat)
Row 1: *K1, p1; rep from * to end.
Row 2: Purl knit stitches and knit purl stitches.

Backward Loop Cast On
Wrap working yarn around thumb, securing the end with your hand. Insert the needle up under the front end of the yarn on the right side of your thumb, making a loop on the needle by pulling on the end of the yarn in your hand.

DIRECTIONS
With circular needles and MC CO 2 sts.
Row 1: K1, p1, blco1 – 3 sts.
Row 2: K1, p1, k1, blco1 – 4 sts.
Row 3: P1tbl, k1, p1, k1, blco1 – 5 sts.
Row 4: P1tbl, k1, p1, k1, p1, blco1 – 6 sts.
Row 5: K1, p1, k1, p1, k1, p1, blco1 – 7 sts.
Row 6: K1, p1, k1, p1, k1, p1, k1, blco1 – 8 sts.

Continue in this manner, working sts in Seed Stitch, using Backward Loop CO to add 1 st to the end of each row. If the first stitch is a purl, purl that stitch through the back loop. Continue until you have 40 sts total. Work 2 rows even in Seed Stitch.

Dec Row: Work in Seed Stitch to last 2 sts, work last 2 sts together in pattern by either p2tog or k2tog – 1 st dec'd. Work this row until 2 sts remain. K2tog – 1 sts. Cut yarn and pull end through remaining loop to secure.

Finishing
Weave in ends, block to make a 8x8" square.

Applied ICord
With circular needle and starting at your BO edge, pick up but do not knit 28 sts along each side of the square – 112 sts.

With CC, CO 2 sts on left needle. K3 – 2 CO sts and the first picked up stitch. Slide these stitches back to left hand needle. *K2, sl 1, k1, psso – 3 sts on right needle. Slip these stitches back to left hand needle. Rep from * until all picked up stitches are worked – 3 sts.

Swich to DPNs and work an icord for 2 ½". Cut yarn leaving a long tail and pull end through remaining stitches. Sew this end to the start of applied icord to attach, and put a little stitch at the top to join the bottom of your hanging loop. Weave in ends and block again to measurements.

MARKET DAY

by The Knit Picks Design Team

Market Day is a fun textured dishcloth worked with knits and purls. It is very easy and is a good choice for beginner knitters. The high relief textures makes for a very useful dishcloth.

FINISHED MEASUREMENTS
9.5" x 9"

YARN
Knit Picks Dishie (worsted weight, 100% cotton, 190 yds/100g): Jalapeno 25785, 1 ball

NEEDLES
US 7 (4.5mm) straight or circular needles, or size to obtain gauge

NOTIONS
Yarn Needle

GAUGE
18 sts and 26 rows = 4" basket weave pattern, blocked

Notes:
Garter stitch (worked flat)
All rows: knit

Basket weave Pattern (worked flat, over a multiple of 6 sts)
Row 1 (RS): knit
Row 2 : purl.
Row 3: *k1, p4, k1, repeat from *.
Row 4: *p1, k4, p1, repeat from *.
Rows 5-6: repeat rows 3-4.
Rows 7-8: repeat rows 1-2.
Row 9: *p2, k2, p2, repeat from *.
Row 10: *k2, p2, k2, repeat from *.
Row 11-12: repeat rows 9-10:

DIRECTIONS
Cast on 44 sts. Work 8 rows in garter sts.

Row 1 (RS): knit
Row 2 : k4, purl to last 4 sts, k4.
Row 3: k4, *k1, p4, k1, repeat from * to last 4 sts, k4.
Row 4: k4, *p1, k4, p1, repeat from * to last 4 sts, k4.
Rows 5-6: repeat rows 3-4.
Rows 7-8: repeat rows 1-2.
Row 9: k4, *p2, k2, p2, repeat from * to last 4 sts, k4
Row 10: k4, *k2, p2, k2, repeat from * to last 4 sts, k4.
Row 11-12: repeat rows 9-10:

Repeat rows 1-12 another 2 times. Repeat Rows 1-7.

Work 7 rows in garter stitch. Bind off.

Finishing
Weave in ends, wash and block gently

SNOWBOBBLES

by Gillian Grimm

The Snowbobbles Dishcloth pattern uses a 5-stitch garter bobble that alternates to a create uniquely textured surface perfect for scrubbing.

FINISHED MEASUREMENTS
8" long x 8" wide.

YARN
Knit Picks Simply Cotton Worsted (100% Organic Cotton; 164 yards/100 grams): Marshmallow, 24761, 1 skein.

NEEDLES
US 6 (4mm) straight or circular needles, or size to obtain gauge

NOTIONS
Yarn Needle

GAUGE
19 sts and 21 rows = 4" in garter stitch.

Notes:

Make Bobble (MB)
Into the stitch where the bobble will be, k1*yo,k1* 2 times. There will now be five sts where there was one. Turn. Knit 5 sts. Turn. K2tog, place stitch just worked back onto left hand needle, pass the remaining 3 sts over the st just worked, one at a time. K1.

DIRECTIONS

Top Border
CO 39 sts

Work 3 rows in garter stitch

Begin Bobble Repeat
Row 1: K3 sts *MB, k3* until 4 sts rem, MB,k3.
Row 2: Knit all sts.
Row 3: K5 sts, *MB, k3* until 2 sts rem, k2.
Row 4: Knit all sts.

Repeat these last 4 rows until the piece measures 7.25 inches from the cast on row.

Bottom Border
Work 3 rows in garter stitch.
BO all stitches.

Finishing
Weave in ends, wash and block to dimensions.

DIAGONAL

by Beth Major

This cloth is designed to aid the beginner crocheter to learn the concepts of increasing and decreasing along the edge of a project and changing yarn colors within a project.

FINISHED MEASUREMENTS
Approximately 8" Square

YARN
Knit Picks CotLin (70% Tanguis Cotton, 30% Linen; 123 yards/50g): MC: Wallaby 25775, CC: Celery 25773, 1 ball each.

HOOKS
US H/8 (5mm)

NOTIONS
Yarn Needle

GAUGE
12 sts = 4" in double crochet (Gauge for this project is approximate)

Notes:

dc2tog – double crochet 2 together
(YO, insert hook in next st and pull up loop, YO and pull through 2 loops on hook, 2 loops left on hook, YO, insert hook in next st and pull up loop, YO and pull through 2 loops on hook, 3 loops left on hook, YO, pull through all loops on hook)

DIRECTIONS
Row 1: With MC, Ch 5, dc in 4th ch from hook, dc in same ch, 2dc in last ch

Row 2: Ch 3, turn, dc in same dc (first dc), dc in each dc across, 2 dc in turning ch.

Row 3 (and every odd number row): Change color, carry unused color along side of work, repeat row 2.

Row 4 and every even number row: Repeat row 2.

Rows 5-12: Increase until the end of 12 rows - 27 sts

Row 13: Change color, carry unused color along side of work. Ch3, turn, dc2tog, dc in each dc across to last 2 sts, dc2tog over the last dc and the turning ch.

Row 14: Ch 3, turn, dc2tog, dc in each dc across to last 2 sts, dc2tog over the last dc and the turning ch.

Row 15 and each odd number row: Repeat row 13

Row 16 and every even number row: Repeat row 14

Decrease until the end of 24 rows – 5 sts. Fasten off.

Finishing
Attach MC with sl st edging color into centre stitch of last 5 sts in last row (should be third st from either edge), ch1, 3 sc in same st, *evenly space 25 sc along side of work, 3 sc in next corner,* repeat between ** 2 times, 25 sc evenly along the last edge, join with sl st to first sc. Fasten off. Weave in ends, wash and block to size.

FEBRUARY

FIELD OF FLOWERS

by The Knit Picks Design Team

Field of Flowers is a very pretty dishcloth or face cloth with a lot of texture. The high relief makes it very efficient for scrubbing.

FINISHED MEASUREMENTS
9" square

YARN
Knit Picks Dishie (100% cotton, 190 yds/100g): Crème Brûlée 25404, 1 ball

NEEDLES
US 7 (4.5mm) straight or circular needles, or size to obtain gauge

NOTIONS
Yarn Needle

GAUGE
21 sts and 26 rows = 4" over daisies patterns, blocked

Notes:
Garter stitch (worked flat)
All rows: knit

Daisies Pattern (worked flat, over a multiple of 4 sts +1)
Row 1 (RS): knit
Row 2 : k1, *Purl next 3 st tog (P3tog), leave sts on left needle, YO, P the same 3 sts tog, drop sts off left needle, k1, repeat from *.
Row 3: knit
Row 4: k1, p1, k1, * Purl next 3 st tog (P3tog), leave sts on left needle, YO, P the same 3 sts tog, drop sts off left needle, k1, repeat from *, end with p1, k1.

DIRECTIONS
Cast on 47 sts. Work 8 rows in garter sts.

Row 1 (RS): knit
Row 2 : k8, *p3tog, yo, p the same 3 sts together again, k1, repeat from *, k7.
Row 3: knit.
Row 4: k8, p1, k1, * p3tog, yo, p the same 3 sts together again, k1, repeat from *, end with p1, k8.

Repeat rows 1-4 another 10 times.

Work 8 rows in garter stitch. Bind off.

Finishing
Weave in ends, wash and block gently

TROPICAL VACATION

by Chelsea Berkompas

This vibrant washcloth pattern makes the most of texture and color with a simple repeated stitch pattern and colorful stripes that will transport you to the tropics while doing your dishes! When switching colors, carry yarns loosely up along the side of the washcloth instead of cutting yarns.

FINISHED MEASUREMENTS
8" square

YARN
Knit Picks Dishie (100% Cotton; 190 yards/100g): MC Begonia 25790, 1 ball; CC Clementine 25403, 1 ball

NEEDLES
US 7 (4.5mm) straight or circular needles, or size to obtain gauge

NOTIONS
Yarn Needle

GAUGE
16 sts and 24 rows = 4" in stitch pattern, unblocked

Notes:
Stitch Pattern (worked flat)
Rows 1-3: Purl all stitches
Row 4: (RS) K1, *YO, Sl 1, K1, Psso; repeat from * to end
Rows 5-7: Purl all stitches
Row 8: (RS) K1, *YO, K2tog; repeat from * to end

Color Pattern
Rows 1-4: MC
Rows 5-8: CC

DIRECTIONS
With MC, loosely CO 33 sts. Work rows 1-4 of stitch pattern.

Join with CC. Work rows 5-8 of stitch pattern.

Repeat these 8 rows 4 times more, continuing the same color pattern.

Ending with row 8, cut CC.

With MC, work rows 1-7 of stitch pattern.

BO loosely, knit-wise.

Finishing
Weave in ends, wash and block if desired

MARITIME FACE CLOTH

by Allison Griffith

The Maritime Facecloth is a generously-sized square of squishy garter stitch bordered by an unbroken cable. Knit in silky Comfy Sport, this washcloth is perfect for even the most delicate skin, and makes a fabulous gift. The Maritime Facecloth is knit on the bias, with two cables worked as you go. To finish, a few stitches of Kitchener stitch join the cables into a beautiful unbroken border.

FINISHED MEASUREMENTS
10" Square

YARN
Knit Picks Comfy Sport (75% Pima Cotton, 25% Acrylic; 136 yards/50g): Sea Foam 24431, 1 ball.

NEEDLES
US 5 (3.75mm) straight or circular needles, or size to obtain gauge

NOTIONS
Yarn Needle
Stitch Markers (2)
Cable Needle
Scrap yarn for provisional cast on

GAUGE
22 sts and 21 ridges = 4" in Garter stitch, unblocked. (Gauge is approximate).

Notes:
This facecloth is cast on at one corner using a provisional cast-on, then knit on the bias. The cable edging is knit at the same time as the garter-stitch center. To finish, a few stitches of Kitchener stitch close up the cast-on and bound-off edges to transform the two separate cables into a single, unbroken border.

3x3 Cable:
Transfer 3 sts onto cable needle. Hold sts in front of work, knit the next 3 sts. Knit 3 sts from cable needle.

Loop Increase (Loop)
Create a loop by wrapping the working yarn around your finger from front to back. Slip your needle into the back part of the loop from the bottom upwards. Tug lightly to tighten st. 1 st inc.

DIRECTIONS
Setup
Using a provisional cast on, CO 12 sts, leaving an 18" tail.
Row 1: P across.
Row 2: 3x3 cable, pm, loop, loop, pm, 3x3 cable.
Row 3: P to first m, sm, k to next m, sm, p to end.

Increase
Row 1: K to first m, sm, loop, k to next m, loop, sm, k to end.
Row 2 (and all even rows): p to first m, sm, k to next m, sm, p to end.
Row 3: K to first m, sm, loop, k to next m, loop, sm, k to end.
Row 5: 3x3 cable, sm, loop, k to next m, loop, sm, 3x3 cable.

Repeat Increase rows 1-6 until you have 68 stitches between the markers.

Decrease
Row 1: K to first m, sm, ssk, k to next m, k2tog, sm, k to end.
Row 3: K to first m, sm, ssk, k to next m, k2tog, sm, k to end.
Row 5: 3x3 cable, sm, ssk, k to next m, k2tog, sm, 3x3 cable.

Repeat Decrease rows 1-6 until you have 4 stitches between the markers (you will end with Decrease Row 4). Then:

Row 1: 3x3 cable, remove m, ssk, k2tog, remove m, 3x3 cable.
Row 2: P5, p2tog ssp, p5.

Finishing
Slip 6. (Your stitches are now arranged evenly on two needles in preparation for the Kitchener stitch.) Break yarn, leaving an 18" tail. Using a yarn needle, join the two cables using the Kitchener stitch to form a continuous cable. Weave in end.

Remove the provisional cast-on from the beginning of the facecloth. Pick up those stitches and repeat the previous step to form one continuous cable all the way around the entire washcloth.

QUEEN OF HEARTS

by Stana D. Sortor

Love is compassion, caring, and a willingness to make something extra special. Why not create a heart shaped dishcloth for yourself or anyone you hold close to your heart? This Queen of Hearts dishcloth contains all knitted rows, and the last stitch at every row is slipped for a nicer edge. Increases and decreases are done on the second and second to last stitches of rows.

FINISHED MEASUREMENTS
10.5" wide, flat x 9.5" high

YARN
Knit Picks Shine Worsted (60% Pima Cotton, 40% Modal; 75 yards/50g): Serrano 24496, 1 ball.

NEEDLES
US 6 (4.25mm) straight or circular needles, or size to obtain gauge

NOTIONS
Yarn Needle

GAUGE
18 sts and 28 rows = 4" in Knit pattern, blocked.

DIRECTIONS
CO 2sts.
Rows 1 – 2: K1, Sl. St.
Row 3: KFB, KFB (4sts total)
Row 4: K3, Sl. st.
Row 5: K1, KFB, KFB, Sl. St. (6sts total)
Row 6: K5, Sl. st.
Row 7: K1, KFB, K2, KFB, Sl. St. (8sts total)
Row 8: K7, Sl. st.
Row 9: K1, KFB, K4, KFB, Sl. St. (10sts total)
Row 10: K9, Sl. st.
Row 11: K1, KFB, K6, KFB, Sl. St. (12sts total)
Row 12: K11, Sl. st.
Row 13: K1, KFB, K8, KFB, Sl. St. (14sts total)
Row 14: K13, Sl. st.
Row 15: K1, KFB, K10, KFB, Sl. St. (16sts total)
Row 16: K15, Sl. st.
Row 17: K1, KFB, K12, KFB, Sl. St. (18sts total)
Row 18: K17, Sl. st.
Row 19: K1, KFB, K14, KFB, Sl. St. (20sts total)
Row 20: K19, Sl. st.
Row 21: K1, KFB, K16, KFB, Sl. St. (22sts total)
Row 22: K21, Sl. st.
Row 23: K1, KFB, K18, KFB, Sl. St. (24sts total)
Row 24: K23, Sl. st.
Row 25: K1, KFB, K20, KFB, Sl. St. (26sts total)
Row 26: K25, Sl. st.
Row 27: K1, KFB, K22, KFB, Sl. St. (28sts total)
Row 28: K27, Sl. st.
Row 29: K1, KFB, K24 KFB, Sl. St. (30sts total)
Row 30: K29, Sl. st.
Row 31: K1, KFB, K26, KFB, Sl. St. (32sts total)
Row 32: K31, Sl. st.
Row 33: K1, KFB, K28, KFB, Sl. St. (34sts total)
Row 34: K33, Sl. st.
Row 35: K1, KFB, K30, KFB, Sl. St. (36sts total)
Row 36: K35, Sl. st.
Row 37: K1, KFB, K32, KFB, Sl. St. (38sts total)
Row 38: K37, Sl. st.
Row 39: K1, KFB, K34, KFB, Sl. St. (40sts total)
Row 40: K39, Sl. st.
Row 41: K1, KFB, K36, KFB, Sl. St. (42sts total)
Row 42: K41, Sl. st.
Row 43: K1, KFB, K38, KFB, Sl. St. (44sts total)
Row 44 – 45: K43, Sl. st.
Row 46: K1, KFB, K40, KFB, Sl. St. (46sts total)
Row 47 – 50: K45, Sl. st.
Row 51: K1, KFB, K42, KFB, Sl. St. (48sts total)
Row 52 – 57: K47, Sl. st.
Row 58: SSK, K43, K2tog, Sl. St. (46sts total)
Row 59 – 62: K45, Sl. st.
Row 63: SSK, K41, K2tog, Sl. St. (44sts total)
Row 64 – 65: K43, Sl. st.
Row 66: SSK, K39, K2tog, Sl. St. (42sts total)
Row 67: K41, Sl. st.

Divide For Top
At this point you will work with first 21sts and leave the last 21sts to work with later.

Row 68: SSK, K16, K2tog, Sl. St. (19sts total), slide next 21 sts to stitch holder to be worked later.
Row 69: SSK, K14, K2tog, Sl. St. (17sts total)
Row 70: SSK, K12, K2tog, Sl. St. (15sts total)
Row 71: SSK, K10, K2tog, Sl. St. (13sts total)
Row 72: SSK, K8, K2tog, Sl. St. (11sts total)
Row 73: SSK, K6, K2tog, Sl. St. (9sts total)
Row 74: SSK, K4, K2tog, Sl. St. (7sts total)
Row 75: Bind off.

Put sts from stitch holder on needle and reattach the yarn at the center of heart. Rep rows 68-75

Finishing
Weave in ends, wash and block to finished measurements

MARCH

KING CHARLES

by The Knit Picks Design Team

King Charles is a fun textured dishcloth worked with knits and purls that looks more complicated than it really is. The diamond relief pattern is surrounded by a seed stitch border for a neat, classic appearance.

FINISHED MEASUREMENTS
9.5" high x 9" wide

YARN
Knit Picks Dishie (100% cotton, 190 yds/100g): Aster 25413, 1 ball

NEEDLES
US 7 (4.5mm) straight or circular needles, or size to obtain gauge

NOTIONS
Yarn Needle

GAUGE
18 sts and 26 rows = 4" over King Charles pattern, blocked.

Notes:
Seed Stitch (worked flat, over an odd number of sts)
All rows: P1, *k1, p1, rep from *.

King Charles pattern (worked flat, over a multiple of 12 sts plus1)
Row 1: K1, *k1, p1, k9, p1, rep from *.
Row 2: K1, *p1, k1, p6, [p1, k1] twice, rep from *.
Row 3: K1, *[k1, p1] twice, k4, [k1, p1] twice, rep from *.
Row 4: P1, (k1, p1) twice, [(p1, k1) twice, p2] 6 times, (k1, p1) 3 times..
Row 5: K1, *k3, [p1, k1] 4 times, k1, rep from *.
Row 6: P1, *p2, [p1, k1] 3 times, p4, rep from *.
Row 7: K1, *k5, p1, k1, p1, k4, rep from *.
Row 8: rep row 6.
Row 9: rep row 5.
Row 10: rep row 4.
Row 11: rep row 3.
Row 12: rep row 2.

DIRECTIONS
CO 47 sts. Work 6 rows in Seed Stitch

Row 1 (RS): P1, (k1, p1) twice, [k1, p1, k9, p1] 3 times, k1, (p1, k1) twice, p1.
Row 2: P1, (k1, p1) twice, [p1, k1, p6, [p1, k1] twice] 3 times, p1, (p1, k1) twice, p1.
Row 3: P1, (k1, p1) twice, [[k1, p1] twice, k4, [k1, p1] twice] 3 times, k1, (p1, k1) twice, p1.
Row 4: P1, (k1, p1) twice, [[p1, k1] twice, p2] twice] 3 times, k1, (p1, k1) twice, p1.
Row 5: P1, (k1, p1) twice, [k3, [p1, k1] 4 times, k1] 3 times, k1, (p1, k1) twice, p1.
Row 6: P1, (k1, p1) twice, [p2, [p1, k1] 3 times, p4] 3 times, k1, (p1, k1) twice, p1.
Row 7: P1, (k1, p1) twice, [k5, p1, k1, p1, k4] 3 times, k1, (p1, k1) twice, p1.
Row 8: rep row 6.
Row 9: rep row 5.
Row 10: rep row 4.
Row 11: rep row 3.
Row 12: rep row 2.

Rep rows 1-12 another 3 times.

Work 6 rows in Seed Stitch. BO all sts..

Finishing
Weave in ends, wash and block gently.

LYDIA'S LILY PAD

by Joyce Fassbender

My mother-in-law, Lydia, was a generous and loving lady. From the beginning, she made me feel like I was part of the family. I designed this cloth for her to say thank you for being so wonderful and for welcoming me so warmly onto her lily pad. This cloth is fully charted and worked in the round. The touch of lace will add lovely decoration to your scrubbing, be it in the kitchen or the bath.

FINISHED MEASUREMENTS
12" diameter

YARN
Knit Picks Shine Sport (60% Pima Cotton, 40% Modal; 110 yards/50g): Green Apple 23617, 1 balll

NEEDLES
US 4 (3.5mm) DPNs and 16 inch circular, or size to obtain gauge

NOTIONS
Yarn Needle

GAUGE
22 sts and 30 rows = 4" stockinette stitch

Notes: This washcloth is worked in the round from the center outward. The cloth is fully charted.

Circular Cast On
Pinch the working yarn between the first and middle finger of your left hand so the end of the yarn comes out behind your fingers. Wrap the working yarn tail around the ring and pinky fingers of your left hand, holding the yarn tail firmly with your right hand. Point the tips of these fingers down toward your palm. *Using your right hand, insert the point of your needle (you can use double points or a circular) under the yarn across the back of your ring and pinky fingers (the 'first loop') from front to back. Pass the needle over the working yarn and draw a loop out from under the first loop; this creates one cast-on stitch. YO.* Repeat from * until you have cast on the required number of stitches. Note: If you need an even number of stitches, you will need to cast on the final stitch as a standard yarn over when you begin your first round of knitting. Arrange the stitches on your double point needles to begin knitting in the round.
Tug on the yarn tail to draw the stitches into a tighter circle.

DIRECTIONS
Cast on 8 stitches using a circular cast on. Place marker and join in the round taking care not to twist stitches.

Row 1: *yo, k1* eight times. 16 sts.
Row 2: knit all stitches

Work Chart
Work all rows as: *Work chart, K1* eight times.

All rows are read from right to left. Switch from DPNs to circular needles as needed.

Finishing
Bind off loosely. Weave in ends, wash and block to finished measurements.

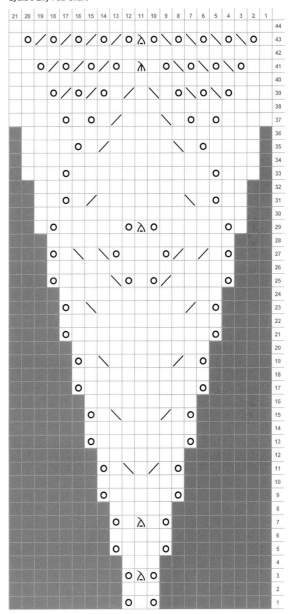

Lydia's Lily Pad Chart

Legend

- **No Stitch** — Placeholder - No stitch made.
- **yo** — Yarn Over
- **knit** — knit stitch
- **sl2, k1, p2sso** — Slip 2 as it to knit, knit 1, pass slipped stitches over knit stitch.
- **k2tog** — Knit two stitches together as one stitch
- **ssk** — Slip another stitch as if to knit. Insert left-hand needle into front of these 2 stitches and knit them together
- **sl1 k2tog psso** — slip 1, k2tog, pass slip stitch over k2tog

LOG CABIN

by Faith Schmidt

This dishcloth is knit in a style called Log Cabin. The central square is knit first, then stitches are picked up, one edge at a time, and the border is knit.

FINISHED MEASUREMENTS
11" square

YARN
Knit Picks Comfy Sport (75% Pima Cotton, 25% Acrylic; 136 yards/50g): C1: Peony 24441, 2 balls; C2: Flamingo 24426, 1 ball.

NEEDLES
US 5 (3.75mm) straight or circular needles, or size to obtain gauge

NOTIONS
Yarn Needle

GAUGE
16.25 sts = 4" in Garter Stitch

Notes: This dishcloth can be knit in any weight yarn, and to any size. To adjust the size, cast on the desired number of sts and then knit the same number of garter ridges. Remember, it takes two rows to make one garter ridge, but the ridges are easier to count in Garter stitch. Continue with instructions as written. The square can also be knit to any size by continuing to repeat the border section until desired size is reached. This is a great place to change colors and use up extra yarn from other projects.

When picking up sts on the side edges, pick them up under the strands between the garter bumps. When picking up sts on the cast on and bound off edges, pick up under each stitch. If after picking up sts, you find you have one stitch more or less than the pattern calls for, don't worry about it. As long as you are picking up sts as described, it should work out fine.

Always bind off and pick up sts on the right side of the work.

Two strands of yarn are held together throughout the pattern.

Garter Stitch (worked flat)
All rows: Knit.

DIRECTIONS
Using 1 strand each of C1 and C2, CO 35 sts.

Knit 35 garter ridges (70 rows).

BO to last st, but do not pull through.

Cut C2, add another strand of C1, so that you are now working with 2 strands of C1, and PU 35 sts along nearest side edge. (36 sts)

Knit 5 garter ridges (10 rows).

BO to last st, but do not pull through.

PU 38 sts along next edge. (39 sts).

Knit 5 garter ridges (10 rows).

BO to last st, but do not pull through.

PU 38 sts along next edge. (39 sts).

Knit 5 garter ridges (10 rows).

BO to last st, but do not pull through.

PU 43 sts along last edge. (44 sts).

Knit 5 garter ridges (10 rows). BO.

Finishing
Weave in ends, block if desired.

GRANNY'S RAINBOW

by Beth Major

Create a colorful splash in your kitchen with a classic stitch pattern in a fun color range. Rotate the center starter color of your Granny's Rainbow dishcloth to create a matching set or use only 2 alternating colors to match your décor.

FINISHED MEASUREMENTS
Approximately 7" square

YARN
Knit Picks CotLin (70% Tanguis Cotton, 30% Linen; 123 yards/50g): Moroccan Red 23996, Clementine 24460, Canary 24837, Sprout 24462, Surf 24459, Nightfall 23991, Blackberry 24467, 1 ball each.

HOOKS
US G/6 (4mm)

NOTIONS
Yarn Needle

GAUGE
16 sts and 8 rows = 4" in dc

DIRECTIONS
With first color, ch 5, join last ch to first ch with sl st to form a ring.

Round 1: Continuing in same color, ch 3 (counts as first dc here and throughout), 2 dc in ring, ch 2, (3dc in ring, ch 2) 3 more times, join with sl st in top ch of initial ch 3, ch 1, fasten off. Do not turn.

Round 2: Join next color with sl st to any ch 2 sp, ch 3, (2dc, ch 2 3 dc) all in same ch 2 sp, (3dc, ch 2, 3dc, ch 1) in each ch 2 sp around, join with sl st in top ch of initial ch 3, ch 1, fasten off. Do not turn.

Round 3: Join next color with sl st to any ch 2 sp, ch 3, (2dc, ch 2 3 dc) all in same ch 2 sp, ch 1, 3 dc in next ch 1 sp, ch 1, (3dc, ch2, 3 dc) in next ch 2 sp, ch , 3 dc in next ch 1 sp, ch 1* repeat from * to * around, join with sl st in top ch of initial ch 3, ch 1, fasten off. Do not turn.

Round 4: Join next color with sl st to any ch 2 sp, ch 3, (2dc, ch 2 3 dc) all in same ch 2 sp, ch 1, (3 dc in next ch 1 sp, ch 1) twice, *(3dc, ch2, 3 dc) in next ch 2 sp, ch 1, (3 dc in next ch 1 sp, ch 1) twice * repeat from * to * around, join with sl st in top ch of initial ch 3, ch 1, fasten off. Do not turn.

Round 5: Join next color with sl st to any ch 2 sp, ch 3, (2dc, ch 2 3 dc) all in same ch 2 sp, ch 1, (3 dc in next ch 1 sp, ch 1) three times, *(3dc, ch2, 3 dc) in next ch 2 sp, ch 1, (3 dc in next ch 1 sp, ch 1) three times* repeat from * to * around, join with sl st in top ch of initial ch 3, ch 1, fasten off. Do not turn.

Round 6: Join next color with sl st to any ch 2 sp, ch 3, (2dc, ch 2 3 dc) all in same ch 2 sp, ch 1, (3 dc in next ch 1 sp, ch 1) four times, *(3dc, ch2, 3 dc) in next ch 2 sp, ch 1, (3 dc in next ch 1 sp, ch 1) four times * repeat from * to * around, join with sl st in top ch of initial ch 3, ch 1, fasten off. Do not turn.

Round 7: Join next color with sl st to any ch 2 sp, ch 3, (2dc, ch 2 3 dc) all in same ch 2 sp, ch 1, (3 dc in next ch 1 sp, ch 1) five times, *(3dc, ch2, 3 dc) in next ch 2 sp, ch 1, (3 dc in next ch 1 sp, ch 1) five times * repeat from * to * around, join with sl st in top ch of initial ch 3, ch 1, fasten off. Do not turn.

Finishing
Weave in all ends, wash, and block to finished size.

APRIL

PETTICOAT

by Kendra Nitta

This project is a great scrap-buster if you have leftover DK or sport weight cotton yarn. The ruffles will become more distinct after washing and drying. Pair with a bar of fancy soap for a thoughtful hostess or teacher gift.

FINISHED MEASUREMENTS
Approximately 9" diameter

YARN
Knit Picks CotLin (70% Tanguis Cotton, 30% Linen; 123 yards/50g): MC Sagebrush 25777, CC1 Whisper 25328, CC2 Raindrop 25326; 1 ball each.

NEEDLES
US 5 (3.75mm) two 16" circular or size to obtain gauge
US 5 (3.75mm) DPNs or two 24" circular needles for two circulars technique, or one 32" or longer circular needle for Magic Loop technique, or size to obtain gauge

NOTIONS
Yarn Needle
Stitch Markers

GAUGE
22 sts and 26 rows = 4" in St st in the round, unblocked. (Gauge for this project is approximate).

Notes:
If you are new to working in the round, a Knitted Cast On may make it easier not to twist your stitches when you join the ends. Knitted Cast On instructions can be found here:
http://tutorials.KnitPicks.com/wptutorials/knitted-cast-on/

The technique for joining the ruffles is very similar to the 3-Needle Bind Off, except that the stitches are left on the needle rather than bound off. Instructions for 3-Needle Bind Off can be found here:
http://tutorials.KnitPicks.com/wptutorials/3-needle-bind-off/

Ruffle Pattern (in the round over an odd number of sts)
Round 1, 3, and 5: *K1, P1, rep from * to last st, K1.
Round 2 and 4: *P1, K1, rep from * to last st, P1.
Round 6: Knit.
Round 7: *K2tog, rep from * to last st, K1.

DIRECTIONS
Outer Ruffle
With MC and one 16" circ needle, CO 239 sts. PM and join into round, taking care not to twist. Work Ruffle Pattern. (120 sts rem) Knit 2 rnds. Next rnd: *K2tog, K6, rep from * to end. (105 sts rem) Knit 1 rnd. Break yarn and set aside. Do not remove sts from needle.

Middle Ruffle
With CC1 and second 16" circ needle, CO 209 sts. PM and join into round, taking care not to twist. Work Ruffle Pattern. (105 sts rem) Knit 1 rnd.

Join Middle Ruffle to Outer Ruffle
Place Outer Ruffle inside Middle Ruffle so that the LH needle for Outer Ruffle is directly behind the LH needle for Middle Ruffle. *Knit first st of Middle Ruffle tog with first st of Outer Ruffle, rep from * to end. Set empty needle aside.

*K2tog, K5, rep from * to end. (90 sts rem). Knit 1 rnd. Break yarn and set aside. Do not remove sts from needle.

Inner Ruffle
With CC2 and first 16" circ needle, CO 179. PM and join into round, taking care not to twist. Work Ruffle Pattern. (90 sts rem) Knit 1 rnd.

Join Inner Ruffle to Middle Ruffle
Place Middle Ruffle inside Inner Ruffle and join as with earlier ruffles. Set empty needle aside. Place markers every 6 sts. Work remaining rounds, changing to DPNs, two circulars, or Magic Loop as needed:

Round 1: *K2tog, knit to m, rep from * to end. (75 sts rem)
Round 2 and 3: Knit.
Round 4: *K2tog, knit to m, rep from * to end. (60 sts rem)
Round 5 and 6: Purl.
Round 7: *P2tog, p to m, rep from * to end. (45 sts rem)
Round 8 and 9: Purl.
Round 10: *P2tog, p to m, rep from * to end. (30 sts rem)
Round 11: Purl.
Round 12: *K2tog, rep from * to end, removing markers as you go. (15 sts rem)
Round 13: *K2tog, k1, rep from * to end. (10 sts rem)
Round 14: *K2tog, rep from * to end. (5 sts rem)
Round 15: K2tog twice, k1. (3 sts rem)

Break yarn, leaving a 10" tail.

Finishing
Using yarn needle, thread yarn tail through remaining sts; tighten to close center.
Weave in ends, wash and block lightly to approximately 9" diameter.

AZTEC

by Kalurah Hudson

This pretty dishcloth is made in Reversible Tapestry Crochet, which creates a dense and sturdy fabric that's ideal for kitchen use. It's crocheted in Comfy Worsted, a creamy blend of pima cotton and acrylic. Make a set of two for the perfect house warming gift!

FINISHED MEASUREMENTS
8" wide x 11" high

YARN
Knit Picks Comfy Worsted (75% Pima Cotton, 25% Acrylic; 109 yards/50g): MC: Hawk 25312, CC: Whisker 24800, 1 ball each.

HOOKS
US G/6 (4mm)

NOTIONS
Yarn Needle
Scissors

GAUGE
16.5 sts and 17 rows = 4" in tapestry single crochet, unblocked

In Tapestry Crochet, you will carry your second color loosely throughout the entire piece of work. You will crochet your working color over the non-working color, letting the second color "float" through the work. Keep your floats nice and loose, however once you reach the end of a row, tighten up the floats just enough to keep them from poking through the work. After pulling them tight, pull on the outsides of your piece to keep an even tension in your work. This will ensure that your dishcloth does not pucker in the middle of the piece.

When working your next color, always finish off the last single crochet of previous color with the new color. This sets up the first loop of your next single crochet in the correct color. Do this at every color change.

Make sure to snug up the first stitch of your new color at every color change but keep the floats nice and loose between changes.

Your first "float" will not occur until row 4 of chart. You can stop carrying your floats after row 44 of chart.

Do not catch or work into any of the floats when crocheting the next row. Floats should do just that, float through the work.

For the edges of your dishcloth, twist your working and contrast color threads at the end of every row. This will give a nice woven appearance to the edges.

DIRECTIONS
Using MC, ch 34.

Row 1 (WS): 1sc in second ch from hook, 1sc in next 32ch. (33 sc)

Row 2: Ch1, turn. 1sc in every sc of row. (33sc)

Row 3-47: Repeat row 2, changing colors as indicated in chart.

Finishing
Weave in ends, block to finished measurements.

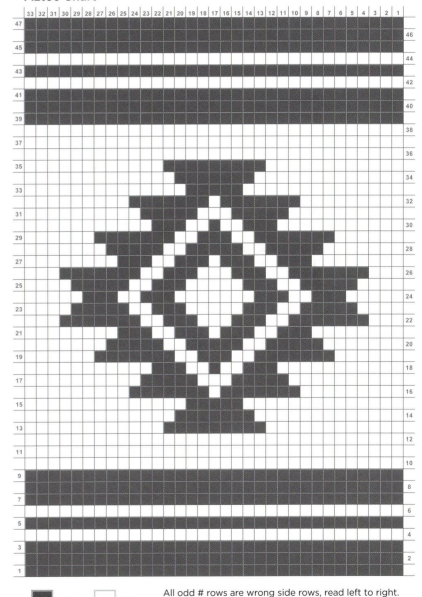

All odd # rows are wrong side rows, read left to right.
All even # rows are right side rows, read right to left.

SHERBET STRIPES

by Gillian Grimm

Bright, delicious stripes, vertical on the front and horizontal on the reverse side, make this dishcloth a welcome addition to your kitchen. A simple 4 row repeat of slip stitches creates a fun color work effect that is deceptively simple to work, but must be done on double pointed needles to allow you to knit from either end of the work.

FINISHED MEASUREMENTS
6" long x 6" wide.

YARN
Knit Picks Dishie (100% Cotton 190 yards/100 grams) MC: Swan, 25409; CC: Clementine, 25403 1 skein each

NEEDLES
5 US (3.75 mm) 2 DPNs, or size to obtain gauge

NOTIONS
Yarn Needle

GAUGE
24 sts and 32 rows = 4 inches bin slip stitch pattern stitch

Notes:

Slip Stitch Pattern (worked over four rows)
Row 1 (RS): With CC, *Sl1 WYIB, k1*, repeat between *'s until 1 st remains, Sl1 WYIB.
Row 2 (WS): Slide the work to the other end of the needle and pick up MC to work. *K1, Sl1 WYIB*, repeat between *'s until 2 st remains, K1. Turn work.
Row 3: With CC, *Sl1 WYIF, P1*, repeat between *s until 1 st remains, Sl1 WYIF.
Row 4: Slide the work to the other end of the needle and pick up MC to work. *P1, Sl1 WYIF*, repeat until 1 st remains, P1. Turn.

DIRECTIONS
With MC, CO 33 sts.

K 1 row.

Begin Slip Stitch Pattern and work 11 rep of the 4 row rep. (44 rows of patt.)

Break CC yarn.

K 1 row in MC.

BO all sts.

Finishing
Weave in ends, wash and block to dimensions.

BUNG GUDNEAU

by Allyson Dykhuizen

The body of the dishcloth is worked corner to corner diagonally, then stitches are picked up around and an applied icord is worked before adding a little loop hanger to finish.

FINISHED MEASUREMENTS
6.5" square measured side to side, 8.5" measured diagonally, 1.25" hanging loop.

YARN
Knit Picks CotLin (70% Tanguis Cotton, 30% Linen; 123 yards/50g): MC: Linen 23995, CC: Sprout 24462; 1 ball each.

NEEDLES
US 5 (3.75mm) 16" circular and 2 DPNs, or size to obtain gauge

NOTIONS
Yarn Needle

GAUGE
20 sts and 32 rows = 4" in Garter Stitch, blocked.

Notes:

Backward Loop Cast On
Wrap working yarn around thumb, securing the end with your hand. Insert the needle up under the front end of the yarn on the right side of your thumb, making a loop on the needle by pulling on the end of the yarn in your hand.

DIRECTIONS
With circular needles and MC CO 2 sts.
Row 1: K2, blco1 – 3 sts.
Row 2: K3, blco1 – 4 sts.
Row 3: K4, blco1 – 5 sts.
Row 4: K5, blco1 – 6 sts.
Continue in this manner, working all stitches in garter stitch and using Backward Loop CO to add 1 st to the end of each row, until you have 40 sts total. Work 2 rows even in garter stitch.

Dec Row: K to last 2 sts, k2tog – 1 st dec'd.
Work this row until 2 sts remain.

Final row: K2tog – 1 st.

Cut yarn and pull end through remaining loop to secure.

Finishing
Weave in ends, block to make a 6x6" square measured side to side, 8" diagonally across dishcloth

Applied ICord
With circular needle and starting at your BO edge, pick up but do not knit 28 sts along each side of the square – 112 sts.

With CC, CO 2 sts on left needle. K3 – 2 CO sts and the first picked up stitch. Slide these stitches back to left hand needle. *K2, sl 1, k1, psso – 3 sts on right needle. Slip these stitches back to left hand needle. Rep from * until all picked up stitches are worked – 3 sts.

Swich to DPNs and work an icord for 2 ½". Cut yarn leaving a long tail and pull end through remaining stitches. Sew this end to the start of applied icord to attach, and put a little stitch at the top to join the bottom of your hanging loop. Weave in ends and block again to measurements.

BICOLOR TWEED

by The Knit Picks Design Team

Bicolor Tweed is a fun, textured dishcloth making the most of two contrasting colors. The pattern is very easy and uses a simple slipped stitch technique, so it's a good choice for beginner knitters. The high relief texture makes for a very useful dishcloth.

FINISHED MEASUREMENTS
9" wide x 8" high

YARN
Knit Picks Dishie (100% cotton, 190 yds/100g): MC: Silver 25789, CC: Fiesta Red 25786; 1 ball each

NEEDLES
US 7 (4.5mm) straight or circular needles, or size to obtain gauge

NOTIONS
Yarn Needle

GAUGE
18 sts and 26 rows = 4" over Bicolor Tweed pattern, blocked.

Notes:

Garter stitch

All rows: knit.

DIRECTIONS
Cast on 41 sts with MC. Work 12 rows in garter stitch.

Row 1 (RS) in CC: K6, *sl1 wyib, k3, repeat from *, k3.

Row 2 in CC: K6, *sl1 wyif, k3, repeat from *, k3.

Row 3 in MC: K4, *sl1 wyib, k3, repeat from *, sl1 wyib, k4.

Row 4 in MC: K4, *sl1 wyif, k3, repeat from *, sl1 wyif, k4.

Repeat rows 1-4 another 12 times.

Work 12 rows in garter stitch. Bind off.

Finishing
Weave in ends, wash and block gently.

CABLED SPA CLOTH

by Beth Major

Learn the basics of crochet cabling with this wonderfully textured spa cloth.

FINISHED MEASUREMENTS
10" square, blocked

YARN
Knit Picks CotLin (70% Tanguis Cotton, 30% Linen; 123 yards/50g): Coffee 24138, 1 ball.

HOOKS
US G/6 (4mm)

NOTIONS
Yarn Needle

GAUGE
9 sts and 6 rows = 2" in HDC

Notes:
Special Stitches
FPdc -Front post double crochet
YO, place your hook in front of your work and then push the hook behind then to the front of the designated stitch, YO and pull up a loop, YO and pull through 2 loops on hook, YO and pull through last 2 loops on hook.

BPdc -Back post double crochet
Place your hook behind your work and then push the hook to the front then behind the designated stitch, YO and pull up a loop, YO and pull through 2 loops on hook, YO and pull through last 2 loops on hook.

FPtr - Front post triple crochet
YO twice, place your hook in front of your work and then push the hook behind then to the front of the designated stitch, YO and pull up a loop, (YO and pull through 2 loops on hook) twice, YO and pull through last 2 loops on hook.

DIRECTIONS
Row 1: Ch 42, turn.

Row 2: Dc in fourth ch from hook and in each ch across – 40 dc

Row 3: ch 2, turn, Hdc in first dc, BPdc around next 2 dc, hdc in next 3 dc, BPdc around next 3 dc, hdc in next 4 dc, BPdc around next 4 dc, hdc in next 2 dc, BPdc around next 2 dc, hdc in next 2 dc, BPdc around next 4 dc, hdc in next 4 dc, BPdc around next 3 dc, hdc in next 3 dc, BPdc around next 2dc, hdc in last st.

Row 4: ch 2, turn, hdc in first hdc, sk next BPdc, FPdc around next BPdc and the skipped BPdc, hdc in next 3 hdc, sk next BPdc, FPdc around next 2 BPdc, FPtr around skipped BPdc, hdc in next 4 hdc, sk next 2 BPdc, FPtr around next 2 BPdc then around skipped BPdc, hdc in next 2 hdc, FPdc around next 2 BPdc, hdc in next 2 hdc, sk next 2 BPdc, FPtr around next 2 BPdc then around skipped BPdc, hdc in next 4 hdc, FPdc around next 2 BPdc, FPtr around skipped BPdc, hdc in next 3 hdc, FPdc around next BPdc and the skipped BPdc, hdc in last hdc,

Row 5: ch 2, turn, hdc in first hdc, BPdc around next 2 FPdc, hdc in next 3 hdc, BPdc around next FPtr and around next 2 FPdc, hdc in next 4 hdc, BPdc around next 4 FPtr, hdc in next 2 hdc, BPdc around next 2 FPdc, hdc in next 2 hdc, BPdc around next 4 FPtr, hdc in next 4 hdc, BPdc around next FPtr and next 2 FPdc, hdc in next 3 hdc, BPdc around next 2 FPdc, hdc in last hdc.

Repeat rows 4 and 5 until cloth measures about 9 inches long, finishing with a row 5.

Finishing
Ch 1, do not turn, 2 sc in last st, evenly space 38 sc along edge, (3 sc in next corner, evenly space 38 sc along next edge) repeat 3 times, join with sl st to first sc. Fasten off and weave in ends, wash and block to diagram.

SOMETHING BLUE

by Joyce Fassbender

When a bride is getting married, tradition holds that she must have something old, something new, something borrowed, and something blue to carry with her down the aisle. On my wedding day, I had managed to fulfill the first three, but nearly panicked when I realized that I didn't have my something blue. Luckily, my brother-in-law was carrying a blue handkerchief that day that he was willing to loan me for the wedding. On the day that my husband and I were weaving our families together, I was aided by the family that had already been woven into mine. The stitch pattern in this dishcloth represents the interweaving of families that happens when a couple chooses to spend their lives together.

FINISHED MEASUREMENTS
9" wide x 8" high

YARN
Knit Picks CotLin (70% Tanguis Cotton, 30% Linen; 123 yards/50g): Nightfall 23991, 1 ball.

NEEDLES
US 6 (4.0mm) straight or circular needles, or size to obtain gauge

NOTIONS
Yarn Needle

GAUGE
24 sts and 28 rows = 4" stockinette stitch.

Notes:
The cloth is charted with a textured center surrounded by a garter stitch edge.

Boxed stitch pattern repeat is worked twice across rows.

DIRECTIONS
Cast on 53 stitches using long tail cast on.

Knit seven (7) rows.

Work Charts

Work Chart A two (2) times.
Odd rows: k5, work chart, k5.
Even rows: k5, work chart, k5.

Work Chart B one (1) time.
Odd rows: k5, work chart, k5.
Even rows: k5, work chart, k5.
After completing chart, knit seven (7) rows.

Finishing
Weave in ends, wash and block to size.

Chart A

Chart B

ZIG ZAG

by Faith Schmidt

Zig Zag dishcloth is a fun and fast knit. The stitch pattern is easy to memorize, and the twisted stitches create a nubbly texture; wonderful for getting your dishes clean. It can easily be resized to fit your needs. Another option is to knit the cloth in a finer yarn on slightly larger needles to make an elegant face cloth.

FINISHED MEASUREMENTS
10" square

YARN
Knit Picks Dishie (100% Cotton; 190 yards/100g): Blush 26668; 1 ball.

NEEDLES
US 7 (4.5mm) straight or circular needles, or size to obtain gauge

NOTIONS
Yarn Needle
Stitch Markers (optional)
Cable Needle

GAUGE
16 sts = 4" over stockinette stitch, unblocked. Exact gauge is not important to this project.

Notes:
To resize, cast on a multiple of 3+4, and knit to desired length.

It took exactly 50 grams to make one dishcloth, so if you were to cast on 46 sts (one less repeat of the stitch pattern), you should be able to get two dishcloths out of one ball.

Crescent Stitch (worked flat)
Row 1(RS): Knit
Row 2 and all even rows: K2, purl to last 2 sts, K2
Row 3: K2, *C3R, repeat from * until last 2 sts, K2
Row 5: K2, *C3L, repeat from * until last 2 sts, K2
Row 6: K2, Purl to last 2 sts, K2

Special Stitches
C3R: Slip 2 sts to a cable needle and hold in back of work, K1, then K2 sts from the cable needle.
C3L: Slip 1 st to a cable needle and hold in front of work, K2, then K1 from the cable needle.

DIRECTIONS
CO 49 sts, using the Long Tail Cast-on.

Knit 1 row.

Work in Crescent Stitch until piece measures approx. 10", or is square, ending with a Row 5.

Knit 1 row (WS). BO in knit.

Finishing
Weave in ends, block if desired.

FISHBONES

by The Knit Picks Design Team

This dishcloth uses a very simple slipped stitch pattern to create a nice diagonal visual effect. It is very easy and is a good choice for beginner knitters or for knitters trying a slipped stitch pattern for the first time. The herringbone pattern makes for a very useful dishcloth.

FINISHED MEASUREMENTS
9.5" wide x9" high

YARN
Knit Picks Dishie (100% cotton, 190 yds/100g): Kenai 25788; 1 ball

NEEDLES
US 7 (4.5mm) straight or circular needles, or size to obtain gauge

NOTIONS
Yarn Needle

GAUGE
18 sts and 26 rows = 4" over Diagonal Herringbone pattern, blocked.

Notes:

Garter stitch

All rows: knit.

Diagonal Herringbone pattern (worked flat, over a multiple of 6 sts)

Row 1 and all odd numbered rows (WS): purl.
Row 2: *sl3, K3; repeat from *.
Row 4: K1, *sl3, K3; repeat from *, end sl3, K2.
Row 6: K2, *sl3, K3; repeat from *, end sl3, K1.
Row 8: *K3, sl3; repeat from *.
Row 10: sl1, *K3, sl3; repeat from *, end K3, sl2.
Row 12: sl2, *K3, sl3; repeat from *, end K3, sl1.

DIRECTIONS
Cast on 46 sts. Work 10 rows in garter stitch

Row 1 and all odd numbered rows (WS): K5 p to last 5 sts, K5.
Row 2: K5, *sl3, K3; repeat from * 6 times, K5.
Row 4: K5, K1, *sl3, K3; repeat from * 5 times, sl3, K2, K5.
Row 6: K5, K2, *sl3, K3; repeat from * 5 times, sl3, K1, K5.
Row 8: K5, *K3, sl3; repeat from * 6 times, K5.
Row 10: K5, sl1, *K3, sl3; repeat from * 5 times, K3, sl2, K5.
Row 12: K5, sl2, *K3, sl3; repeat from * 5 times, K3, sl1, K5.

Repeat rows 1-12 another 3 times.

Work 10 rows in garter stitch. Bind off.

Finishing
Weave in ends, wash and block gently.

JUNE

PINWHEEL

by Allison Griffith

This dishcloth is a cheerful little project with vintage flare. Based on a traditional American quilt block pattern, it is a fantastic way to play with color and use up scraps. The Pinwheel Dishcloth is cast on between a Main Color and a Contrast Color section using the provisional cast on. Using short-rows and wrap-and-turns, the washcloth is knit to form a square, and finished with a few stitches of Kitchener stitch.

FINISHED MEASUREMENTS
7" square

YARN
Knit Picks Dishie (100% Cotton; 190 yards/100g): MC-Swan 25409, CC1-Mulberry 25784, CC2-Begonia 25790, CC3-Crème Brûlée 25404, CC4-Kenai 25788; 1 ball each.

NEEDLES
US 7 (4.5mm) straight or circular needles, or size to obtain gauge

NOTIONS
Yarn Needle
Scrap yarn for provisional cast on

GAUGE
18 sts and 17 ridges = 4" in Garter stitch, unblocked. (Gauge is approximate)

Notes:
This dishcloth is cast on between a Main Color and a Contrast Color section using the provisional cast on. Using short-rows and wrap-and-turns, the washcloth is knit back and forth to form a square. After the last section is knit, the Kitchener stitch is used to join the remaining active stitches to the original provisional cast-on stitches.

DIRECTIONS
Setup
Using a provisional cast on, CO 16 sts, leaving an 24" tail.

MC Section
Using MC, work as follows, ending with an even row.

Row 1: K15, w&t.
Row 2: (and all even-numbered rows) Knit.
Row 3: K14, w&t.
Row 5: K13, w&t.
Row 7: K12, w&t.
Row 9: K11, w&t.
Row 11: K10, w&t.
Row 13: K9, w&t.
Row 15: K8, w&t.
Row 17: K7, w&t.
Row 19: K6, w&t.
Row 21: K5, w&t.
Row 23: K4, w&t.
Row 25: K3, w&t.
Row 27: K2, w&t.

CC Section
Break MC yarn, and join CC1, CC2, CC3, or CC4. Work as follows, ending with an even row.

Row 1: Knit 3, knitting wrap with the last stitch.
Row 2: (and all even-numbered rows) Slp 1 knitwise, k to end.
Row 3: Knit 4, knitting wrap with the last stitch.
Row 5: Knit 5, knitting wrap with the last stitch.
Row 7: Knit 6, knitting wrap with the last stitch.
Row 9: Knit 7, knitting wrap with the last stitch.
Row 11: Knit 8, knitting wrap with the last stitch.
Row 13: Knit 9, knitting wrap with the last stitch.
Row 15: Knit 10, knitting wrap with the last stitch.
Row 17: Knit 11, knitting wrap with the last stitch.
Row 19: Knit 12, knitting wrap with the last stitch.
Row 21: Knit 13, knitting wrap with the last stitch.
Row 23: Knit 14, knitting wrap with the last stitch.
Row 25: Knit 15, knitting wrap with the last stitch.
Row 27: Knit 16, knitting wrap with the last stitch.

Work MC and CC Sections 3 more times. Be sure to alternate CC1-4 for the CC Section.

End with Row 28 of CC Section.

Finishing
Remove the provisional cast-on, and use the MC tail to sew the live stitches of the cast-on edge to the live stitches from the end of the last CC Section. Use Kitchener Stitch to continue the garter stitch pattern.

Weave in ends and block lightly.

CAERPHILLY

by Allyson Dykhuizen

Caerphilly, a moated medieval castle in South Wales, is represented here with heraldry chevron texture and applied i-cord "moat." But really, this is just a fun textured dishcloth and a reason for you to wiki search Caerphilly!

FINISHED MEASUREMENTS
7.5" square measured side to side, 9.5" measured diagonally, 1.25" hanging loop.

YARN
Knit Picks CotLin (70% Tanguis Cotton, 30% Linen; 123 yards/50g): Crème Brulee (MC) 24137, Harbor (CC) 24464; 1 ball each.

NEEDLES
US 5 (3.75mm) 16" circular and 2 DPNs, or size to obtain gauge

NOTIONS
Yarn Needle

GAUGE
22 sts and 28 rows = 4" in Little Chevron Rib, blocked.

Notes:
The body of the dishcloth is worked, then stitches are picked up around and an applied icord is worked before adding a little loop hanger is added to finish.

Little Chevron Rib
Row 1 (RS): P1, *k1, p1, [k2, p1] twice, k1, p1; rep from * to end.
Row 2 (WS): K1, *p2, [k1, p1] twice, k1, p2, k1; rep from * to end.
Row 3: P1, *k3, p3, k3, p1; rep from * to end.
Row 4: K2, *p3, k1, p3, k3; rep from * to last 9 sts, p3, k1, p3, k2.
Rep these 4 rows for pattern.

DIRECTIONS
With circular needles and MC CO 41 sts. Work in Little Chevron Rib, completing 4 row pattern repeat 12 times. BO.

Cut yarn and pull end through remaining loop to secure.

Finishing
Weave in ends, block to make a 7x7" square measured side to side, 9" diagonally across dishcloth.

Applied ICord
With circular needle and starting at your BO edge, pick up but do not knit 28 sts along each side of the square – 112 sts.

With CC, CO 2 sts on left needle. K3 – 2 CO sts and the first picked up stitch. Slide these stitches back to left hand needle. *K2, sl 1, k1, psso – 3 sts on right needle. Slip these stitches back to left hand needle. Rep from * until all picked up stitches are worked – 3 sts.

Switch to DPNs and work an icord for 2 ½". Cut yarn leaving a long tail and pull end through remaining stitches. Sew this end to the start of applied icord to attach, and put a little stitch at the top to join the bottom of your hanging loop. Weave in ends and block again to measurements.

SIMPLE LINES

by Chelsea Berkompas

Sometimes simple is best. This dishcloth pattern is just that: simple vertical ribs of varying widths with a little garter stitch border. The perfect dishcloth for brand new knitters who wish to practice their knits and purls, or for anyone who appreciates a good, stretchy, simple dishcloth.

FINISHED MEASUREMENTS
8" square

YARN
Knit Picks Dishie (100% Cotton; 190 yards/50g): Silver 25789; 1 ball.

NEEDLES
US 5 (3.75mm) straight or circular needles, or size to obtain gauge

NOTIONS
Yarn Needle

GAUGE
18 sts and 26 rows = 4" in ribbed stitch pattern, stretched to measurements.

Notes:
Stitch Pattern (worked flat)
Row 1 (RS): P2, K4, P2, K3, P2, K2, P2, K1, P2, K2, P2, K3, P2, K4, P2
Row 2 (WS): P6, K2, P3, K2, P2, K2, P1, K2, P2, K2, P3, K2, P6

DIRECTIONS
Loosely CO 35 sts.

Work rows 1 and 2 of stitch pattern, repeating 27 times for a total of 54 rows, ending on WS.

On RS, loosely BO all stitches.

Finishing
Weave in ends, wash and block if desired

SQUARE CHECK

by The Knit Picks Design Team

Square Check is a fun textured dishcloth worked with knits and purls. It is very easy and is a good choice for beginner knitters. The geometric pattern makes for a very pretty dishcloth or face cloth.

FINISHED MEASUREMENTS
8.5x8"

YARN
Knit Picks Dishie (100% cotton, 190 yds/100g): Blush 26668; 1 ball

NEEDLES
US 7 (4.5mm) straight or circular needles, or size to obtain gauge

NOTIONS
Yarn Needle

GAUGE
18 sts and 26 rows = 4" over Squared Check pattern, blocked..

Notes: The Knitted Cast On tutorial is here: http://tutorials.KnitPicks.com/wptutorials/knitted-cast-on/

Notes:
Garter stitch
All rows: knit.

Squared Check pattern (worked flat, over a multiple of 10 sts plus 2)
Row 1: knit.
Row 2: purl.
Row 3: k2, *p8, k2, repeat from *.
Row 4: p2, *k8, p2, repeat from *.
Row 5: k2, *p2, k4, p2, k2, repeat from *.
Row 6: p2, *k2, p4, k2, p2, repeat from *.
Row 7: repeat row 5.
Row 8: repeat row 6.
Row 9: repeat row 5.
Row 10: repeat row 6.
Row 11: repeat row 3.
Row 12: repeat row 4.

DIRECTIONS
CO 44 sts. Work 12 rows in garter st

Row 1 (RS): knit.
Row 2: k6, purl to last 6 sts, k6.
Row 3: k8, *p8, k2, repeat from *, k6.
Row 4: k6, p2, *k8, p2, repeat from *, k6.
Row 5: k8, *p2, k4, p2, k2, repeat from *, k6.
Row 6: k6, p2, *k2, p4, k2, p2, repeat from *, k6.
Row 7: repeat row 5.
Row 8: repeat row 6.
Row 9: repeat row 5.
Row 10: repeat row 6.
Row 11: repeat row 3.
Row 12: repeat row 4.

Repeat rows 1-12 another 3 times.

Work 12 rows in garter stitch. BO all sts.

Finishing
Weave in ends and block if desired.

JULY

LOVE MUSIC

by Erica Jackofsky

This dishcloth makes a great quick gift knit for your favorite music lover or teacher. Choose a lighter color yarn to show off the reverse stockinette patterning to the greatest extent. The pattern is both written out and charted.

FINISHED MEASUREMENTS
Approximately 10" Square

YARN
Knit Picks Dishie (worsted weight, 100% cotton, 190 yds/100g): Linen 25400, 1 ball.

NEEDLES
US 6 (4mm) straight or circular needles, or size to obtain gauge

NOTIONS
Yarn Needle

GAUGE
20 sts and 25 rows = 4" in Stockinette Stitch blocked. .

Notes:
Garter stitch
All rows: knit.

Seed Stitch (worked flat)
Row 1: *K1, P1; rep from * across row.
Row 2: *P1, K1; rep from * across r

DIRECTIONS
CO 52 sts.
Rows 1-4: Work 4 rows in seed stitch.
Row 5: (k1, p1) 2 times, k45, p1, k1, p1
Row 6: (p1, k1) 2 times, p45, k1, p1, k1
Row 7: (k1, p1) 2 times, k25, p2, k18, p1, k1, p1
Row 8: (p1, k1) 2 times, p16, k4, p25, k1, p1, k1
Row 9: (k1, p1) 2 times, k24, p5, k16, p1, k1, p1
Row 10: (p1, k1) 2 times, p14, k7, p24, k1, p1, k1
Row 11: (k1, p1) 2 times, k22, p4, k1, p4, k14, p1, k1, p1
Row 12: (p1, k1) 2 times, p12, k4, p2, k5, p22, k1, p1, k1
Row 13: (k1, p1) 2 times, k20, p3, k1, p2, k3, p3, k13, p1, k1, p1
Row 14: (p1, k1) 2 times, p12, k2, p4, k2, p2, k4, p19, k1, p1, k1
Row 15: (k1, p1) 2 times, k17, p4, k3, p3, k3, p2, k13, p1, k1, p1
Row 16: (p1, k1) 2 times, p12, k2, p2, k4, p4, k4, p17, k1, p1, k1
Row 17: (k1, p1) 2 times, k15, p4, k6, p4, k1, p2, k13, p1, k1, p1
Row 18: (p1, k1) 2 times, p12, k7, p7, k4, p15, k1, p1, k1
Row 19: (k1, p1) 2 times, k13, p4, k10, p5, k13, p1, k1, p1
Row 20: (p1, k1) 2 times, p10, k6, p11, k5, p13, k1, p1, k1
Row 21: (k1, p1) 2 times, k11, p5, k13, p6, k10, p1, k1, p1
Row 22: (p1, k1) 2 times, p8, k6, p15, k5, p11, k1, p1, k1
Row 23: (k1, p1) 2 times, k9, p6, k15, p7, k8, p1, k1, p1
Row 24: (p1, k1) 2 times, p6, k5, p1, k2, p16, k5, p10, k1, p1, k1
Row 25: (k1, p1) 2 times, k9, p4, k17, p2, k3, p4, k6, p1, k1, p1
Row 26: (p1, k1) 2 times, p5, k3, p4, k2, p17, k5, p2, k2, p5, k1, p1, k1
Row 27: (k1, p1) 2 times, k3, p4, k1, p5, k15, p5, k4, p3, k5, p1, k1, p1
Row 28: (p1, k1) 2 times, p4, k3, p3, k7, p3, k4, p7, k5, p1, k4, p4, k1, p1, k1
Row 29: (k1, p1) 2 times, k4, p2, k2, p5, k6, p6, k1, p9, k3, p3, k4, p1, k1, p1
Row 30: (p1, k1) 2 times, p3, k3, p2, k3, p1, k2, p1, k11, p5, k5, p9, k1, p1, k1
Row 31: (k1, p1) 2 times, k8, p5, k5, p10, k2, p2, k2, p2, k2, p3, k4, p1, k1, p1
Row 32: (p1, k1) 2 times, p3, k3, p2, k2, p2, k2, p3, k8, p6, k5, p9, k1, p1, k1
Row 33: (k1, p1) 2 times, k4, p2, k2, p5, k7, p7, k3, p2, k2, p2, k2, p3, k4, p1, k1, p1
Row 34: (p1, k1) 2 times, p3, k3, p2, k2, p2, k2, p3, k4, p10, k4, p2, k4, p4, k1, p1, k1
Row 35: (k1, p1) 2 times, k3, p4, k2, p5, k9, p4, k3, p2, k1, p2, k3, p3, k4, p1, k1, p1
Row 36: (p1, k1) 2 times, p4, k3, p3, k4, p2, k3, p1, k3, p6, k5, p4, k2, p5, k1, p1, k1
Row 37: (k1, p1) 2 times, k11, p12, k3, p3, k1, p2, k3, p4, k6, p1, k1, p1
Row 38: (p1, k1) 2 times, p6, k11, p5, k9, p14, k1, p1, k1
Row 39: (k1, p1) 2 times, k15, p4, k9, p9, k8, p1, k1, p1
Row 40: (p1, k1) 2 times, p9, k6, p30, k1, p1, k1
Row 41: (k1, p1) 2 times, k30, p2, k13, p1, k1, p1
Row 42: (p1, k1) 2 times, p12, k2, p31, k1, p1, k1
Row 43: (k1, p1) 2 times, k30, p2, k13, p1, k1, p1
Row 44: (p1, k1) 2 times, p12, k2, p31, k1, p1, k1
Row 45: (k1, p1) 2 times, k30, p2, k13, p1, k1, p1
Row 46: (p1, k1) 2 times, p12, k2, p31, k1, p1, k1
Row 47: (k1, p1) 2 times, k30, p2, k4, p3, k6, p1, k1, p1
Row 48: (p1, k1) 2 times, p4, k5, p3, k2, p31, k1, p1, k1
Row 49: (k1, p1) 2 times, k30, p2, k3, p5, k5, p1, k1, p1
Row 50: (p1, k1) 2 times, p4, k5, p3, k2, p31, k1, p1, k1
Row 51: (k1, p1) 2 times, k30, p2, k4, p3, k6, p1, k1, p1
Row 52: (p1, k1) 2 times, p5, k2, p4, k3, p31, k1, p1, k1
Row 53: (k1, p1) 2 times, k31, p8, k6, p1, k1, p1
Row 54: (p1, k1) 2 times, p6, k6, p33, k1, p1, k1
Row 55: (k1, p1) 2 times, k33, p4, k8, p1, k1, p1
Row 56: (p1, k1) 2 times, p45, k1, p1, k1
Row 57: (k1, p1) 2 times, k45, p1, k1, p1
Row 58: (p1, k1) 2 times, p45, k1, p1, k1
Rows 59-62: Work 4 rows in seed stitch.
BO all sts.

Finishing
Weave in ends, wash and block as necessary.

Legend

knit
☐ RS: knit stitch
WS: purl stitch

purl
● RS: purl stitch
WS: knit stitch

TAJ

by Joyce Fassbender

The cloth has a beautiful cabled medallion center, surrounded by a garter background with a braided cable edge.

FINISHED MEASUREMENTS
8" wide x 9" high

YARN
Knit Picks CotLin (70% Tanguis Cotton, 30% Linen; 123 yards/50g):Whisker 24834; 1 ball.

NEEDLES
US 5 (3.75mm) straight or circular needles, or size to obtain gauge

NOTIONS
Yarn Needle

GAUGE
26 sts and 32 rows = 4" garter stitch.

Notes:
Special Abbreviations

23rkc: slip 3 on cn, hold to back, k2, k3 sts from cn

32rpc: slip 2 on cn, hold to back, p3, p2 sts from cn

c2b: slip 1 on cn, hold to back, k1, k1 st from cn

c2f: slip 1 on cn, hold to front, k1, k1 st from cn

c4b: slip 2 on cn, hold to back, k2, k2 sts from cn

c4f: slip 2 on cn, hold to front, k2, k2 sts from cn

p2sso: pass two slipped stitches over

s2: slip two stitches knitwise onto right needle

DIRECTIONS
Cast on 55 stitches using long tail cast on.

Row 1: c2b, k1, m1, k5, s2, k1, p2sso, k7, m1, k1, m1, k7, s2, k1, p2sso, k7, m1, k1, m1, k7, s2, k1, p2sso, k5, m1, k1, c2f

Row 2: p3, k49, p3

Row 3: k1, c2f, m1, k5, s2, k1, p2sso, k7, m1, k1, m1, k7, s2, k1, p2sso, k7, m1, k1, m1, k7, s2, k1, p2sso, k5, m1, c2b, k1

Row 4: p3, k49, p3

Row 5: c2b, k1, m1, k5, s2, k1, p2sso, k7, m1, k1, m1, k7, s2, k1, p2sso, k7, m1, k1, m1, k7, s2, k1, p2sso, k5, m1, k1, c2f

Row 6: p3, k49, p3

Row 7: k1, c2f, m1, k5, s2, k1, p2sso, k7, m1, k1, m1, k7, s2, k1, p2sso, k7, m1, k1, m1, k7, s2, k1, p2sso, k5, m1, c2b, k1

Row 8: p3, k49, p3

Row 9: c2b, k51, c2f

Row 10: p3, k49, p3

Row 11: k1, c2f, k22, 23rkc, k22, c2b, k1

Row 12: p3, k22, p2, k1, p2, k22, p3

Row 13: c2b, k21, c4b, k1, c4f, k21, c2f

Row 14: p3, k20, p4, k1, p4, k20, p3

Row 15: k1, c2f, k18, c4b, k5, c4f, k18, c2b, k1

Row 16: p3, k6, p4, k8, p2, k2, p2, k1, p2, k2, p2, k8, p4, k6, p3

Row 17: c2b, k5, c4b, c4f, k4, c4b, k9, c4f, k4, c4b, c4f, k5, c2f

Row 18: p3, k4, p2, k4, p2, k4, p4, k2, p2, k1, p2, k2, p4, k4, p2, k4, p2, k4, p3

Row 19: k1, c2f, k2, c4b, k4, c4f, c4b, k13, c4f, c4b, k4, c4f, k2, c2b, k1

Row 20: p3, k2, p2, k8, p4, k2, p2, k2, p2, k1, p2, k2, p2, k2, p4, k8, p2, k2, p3

Row 21: c2b, k13, c4f, k17, c4b, k13, c2f

Row 22: p3, k2, p2, k10, p2, k2, p2, k2, p2, k1, p2, k2, p2, k2, p2, k10, p2, k2, p3

Row 23: k1, c2f, k2, c4f, k37, c4b, k2, c2b, k1

Row 24: p3, k4, p2, k8, p2, k2, p2, k2, p2, k1, p2, k2, p2, k2, p2, k8, p2, k4, p3

Row 25: c2b, k5, c4f, k12, c4b, k1, c4f, k12, c4b, k5, c2f

Row 26: p3, k6, p2, k6, p2, k2, p4, k5, p4, k2, p2, k6, p2, k6, p3

Row 27: k1, c2f, k6, c4f, k6, c4b, k9, c4f, k6, c4b, k6, c2b, k1

Row 28: p3, k8, p2, k4, p4, k2, p2, k5, p2, k2, p4, k4, p2, k8, p3

Row 29: c2b, k7, c4b, k2, c4b, k17, c4f, k2, c4f, k7, c2f

Row 30: p3, k6, p2, k4, p2, k2, p2, k2, p2, k5, p2, k2, p2, k2, p2, k4, p2, k6, p3

Row 31: k1, c2f, k4, c4b, k12, c4f, k1, c4b, k12, c4f, k4, c2b, k1

Row 32: p3, k4, p2, k6, p2, k2, p2, k2, p2, k1, p2, k2, p2, k2, p2, k6, p2, k4, p3

Row 33: c2b, k3, c4b, k37, c4f, k3, c2f

Row 34: p3, k2, p2, k8, p2, k2, p2, k4, 32rpc, k4, p2, k2, p2, k8, p2, k2, p3

Row 35: k1, c2f, k2, c4f, k37, c4b, k2, c2b, k1

Row 36: p3, k4, p2, k6, p2, k2, p2, k2, p2, k1, p2, k2, p2, k2, p2, k6, p2, k4, p3

Row 37: c2b, k5, c4f, k12, c4b, k1, c4f, k12, c4b, k5, c2f

Row 38: p3, k6, p2, k4, p2, k2, p2, k2, p2, k5, p2, k2, p2, k2, p2, k4, p2, k6, p3

Row 39: k1, c2f, k6, c4f, k2, c4f, k17, c4b, k2, c4b, k6, c2b, k1

Row 40: p3, k8, p2, k4, p4, k2, p2, k5, p2, k2, p4, k4, p2, k8, p3

Row 41: c2b, k7, c4b, k6, c4f, k9, c4b, k6, c4f, k7, c2f

Row 42: p3, k6, p2, k6, p2, k2, p4, k5, p4, k2, p2, k6, p2, k6, p3

Row 43: k1, c2f, k4, c4b, k12, c4f, k1, c4b, k12, c4f, k4, c2b, k1

Row 44: p3, k4, p2, k8, p2, k2, p2, k2, p2, k1, p2, k2, p2, k2, p2, k8, p2, k4, p3

Row 45: c2b, k3, c4b, k37, c4f, k3, c2f

Row 46: p3, k2, p2, k10, p2, k2, p2, k2, p2, k1, p2, k2, p2, k2, p2, k10, p2, k2, p3

Row 47: k1, c2f, k12, c4b, k17, c4f, k12, c2b, k1

Row 48: p3, k2, p2, k8, p4, k2, p2, k2, p2, k1, p2, k2, p2, k2, p4, k8, p2, k2, p3

Row 49: c2b, k3, c4f, k4, c4b, c4f, k13, c4b, c4f, k4, c4b, k3, c2f

Row 50: p3, k4, p2, k4, p2, k4, p4, k2, p2, k1, p2, k2, p4, k4, p2, k4, p2, k4, p3

Row 51: k1, c2f, k4, c4f, c4b, k4, c4f, k9, c4b, k4, c4f, c4b, k4, c2b, k1

Row 52: p3, k6, p4, k8, p2, k2, p2, k1, p2, k2, p2, k8, p4, k6, p3
Row 53: c2b, k19, c4f, k5, c4b, k19, c2f
Row 54: p3, k20, p4, k1, p4, k20, p3
Row 55: k1, c2f, k20, c4f, k1, c4b, k20, c2b, k1
Row 56: p3, k22, p5, k22, p3
Row 57: c2b, k23, 23rkc, k23, c2f
Row 58: p3, k49, p3
Row 59: k1, c2f, k49, c2b, k1
Row 60: p3, k49, p3
Row 61: c2b, k1, k2tog, k4, m1, k1, m1, k7, s2, k1, p2sso, k7, m1, k1, m1, k7, s2, k1, p2sso, k7, m1, k1, m1, k4, ssk, k1, c2f
Row 62: p3, k49, p3
Row 63: k1, c2f, k2tog, k4, m1, k1, m1, k7, s2, k1, p2sso, k7, m1, k1, m1, k7, s2, k1, p2sso, k7, m1, k1, m1, k4, ssk, c2b, k1
Row 64: p3, k49, p3
Row 65: c2b, k1, k2tog, k4, m1, k1, m1, k7, s2, k1, p2sso, k7, m1, k1, m1, k7, s2, k1, p2sso, k7, m1, k1, m1, k4, ssk, k1, c2f
Row 66: p3, k49, p3
Row 67: k1, c2f, k2tog, k4, m1, k1, m1, k7, s2, k1, p2sso, k7, m1, k1, m1, k7, s2, k1, p2sso, k7, m1, k1, m1, k4, ssk, c2b, k1
Row 68: p3, k49, p3

Loosely bind off all stitches.

Finishing

Weave in ends, wash and block to size.

CHECKS AND EYELETS

by Faith Schmidt

The Checks and Eyelets facecloth is a quick and fun knit. The stitch pattern is easy to memorize, and the eyelets create a lacy texture; perfect for gift giving, or just for pampering yourself. It can easily be resized to fit your needs.

FINISHED MEASUREMENTS
Approx. 10" square, blocked

YARN
Knit Picks CotLin (70% Cotton, 30% Linen; 123 yards/50g): Surf 24459; 1 ball

NEEDLES
US 4 (4.5mm) straight or circular needles, or size to obtain gauge

NOTIONS
Yarn Needle

GAUGE
18 sts = 4" over stockinette stitch, unblocked. Exact gauge is not important to this project.

Notes:
To resize, cast on a multiple of 6+4, and knit to desired length..

Checks and Eyelets Stitch (worked flat)
Rows 1 (RS), 2, 3, 4: K2, *K3, P3, repeat from * to last 2 sts, K2
Row 5: K2, *YO, SL1, K2TOG, PSSO, YO, K3, repeat from * to last 2 sts, K2
Rows 6, 7, 8, 9, 10: K2, *P3, K3, repeat from * to last 2 sts, K2
Row 11: K2, *K3, YO, SL1, K2TOG, PSSO, YO, repeat from * to last 2 sts, K2
Row 12: K2, *K3, P3, repeat from * to last 2 sts, K2

Special Stitches
SL1, K2TOG, PSSO: Slip 1 st knitwise, knit the next 2 sts together, pass the slipped st over the decreased sts, and off the needle.

DIRECTIONS
CO 40 sts using the Long Tail Cast-on.

Knit 3 rows (2 garter ridges on RS).

Work Checks and Eyelets Stitch (Rows 1-12) 5 times total, then work Rows 1 and 2 once.

Knit 3 rows.

BO (WS) in knit.

Finishing
Weave in ends, block if desired.

HAPPY SHEEP

by Chelsea Berkompas

Everyone needs a dishcloth featuring a sheep! Simply a combination of knits and purls, the Happy Sheep motif is easy to knit and is finished off with a garter stitch border. Knit in the soft yet hardworking Comfy Worsted, this is one dishcloth that will keep you and your kitchen smiling!

FINISHED MEASUREMENTS
7x9"

YARN
Knit Picks Comfy Worsted (75% Pima Cotton, 25% Acrylic; 109 yards/50g): Ivory 24162; 1 ball.

NEEDLES
US 8 (5mm) straight or circular needles, or size to obtain gauge

NOTIONS
Yarn Needle

GAUGE
20 sts and 24 rows = 4" in Stockinette Stitch

DIRECTIONS
Loosely CO 41 sts.

Rows 1-5: K all stitches.
Row 6 (RS): K3, P35, K3.
Row 7 (WS): K all stitches.
Row 8: Rep row 6.
Row 9: Rep row 7.
Row 10: K3, P12, K2, P11, K2, P8, k3.
Row 11: K11, P2, K11, P2, K15.
Row 12: K3, P12, K2, P11, K2, P8, K3.
Row 13: Rep row 11.
Row 14: K3, P10, K18, P7, K3.
Row 15: K8, P22, K11.
Row 16: K3, P7, K24, p4, K3.
Row 17: K7, P24, K10.
Row 18: Rep row 16.
Row 19: Rep row 17.
Row 20: Rep row 16.
Row 21: Rep row 17.
Row 22: Rep row 16.
Row 23: Rep row 17.
Row 24: K3, P2, K31, P2, K3.
Row 25: K5, P31, K5.
Row 26: Rep row 24.
Row 27: K7, P29, K5.
Row 28: K3, P3, K27, P5, K3.
Row 29: K10, P24, K7.
Row 30: K3, P5, K23, P7, K3.
Row 31: K27, P6, K8.
Row 32: K3, P6, K4, P25, K3.
Row 33: K28, P1, K2, P1, K8.
Row 34: K3, P5, K1, P2, K1, P26, K3.
Row 35: K all stitches.
Row 36: K3, P35, K3.
Row 37: Rep row 35.
Row 38: Rep row 36.
Rows 39-43: K all stitches.

On next row, BO all stitches loosely. Cut yarn.

.Finishing
Weave in ends, wash and block if desired

CAMPFIRE

by The Knit Picks Design Team

Campfire is a fun textured dishcloth worked using slipped stitches. The chevron pattern resembles flames sparking up into the night. This easy, beginner-friendly dishcloth will light up any kitchen!

FINISHED MEASUREMENTS
9.5" wide x9" high

YARN
Knit Picks Dishie (100% cotton, 190 yds/100g): Clementine 25403; 1 ball

NEEDLES
US 7 (4.5mm) straight or circular needles, or size to obtain gauge

NOTIONS
Yarn Needle

GAUGE
20 sts and 32 rows = 4" over Campfire pattern, blocked. .

Notes:

Garter stitch
All rows: knit.

Campfire pattern
Row 1: k2, *p5, k3, repeat from * end with p5, k2.
Row 2: k2, *sl5 WYIF, k3, repeat from *, end with sl5 WYIF, k2.
Row 3: repeat row 1
Row 4: k4, *insert needle under loose strand and knit next st, bringing st out under strand; k7, repeat from *, end last repeat with k4.

DIRECTIONS
Cast on 47 sts. Work 6 rows in garter stitch.

Row 1: k5, *p5, k3, repeat from * end with p5, k5.
Row 2: k5, *sl5 WYIF, k3, repeat from *, end with sl5 WYIF, k5.
Row 3: repeat row 1
Row 4: k7, *insert needle under loose strand and knit next st, bringing st out under strand; k7, repeat from *, end last repeat with k7.

Repeat rows 1-4 another 16 times.

Work 6 rows in garter stitch. Bind off.

Finishing
Weave in ends, wash and block gently.

BELOEIL

by Allyson Dykhuizen

The Chateau de Beloeil is a big castle in Belgium surrounded by a moat, much like this dishcloth's Herringbone stitch is surrounded by applied icord. A stretch? Well hey! You just learned about a beautiful castle in Belgium, so just roll with it!

FINISHED MEASUREMENTS
7.5" square measured side to side, 9.5" measured diagonally, 1 ¼" hanging loop.

YARN
Knit Picks CotLin (70% Tanguis Cotton, 30% Linen; 123 yards/50g): Harbor (MC) 24464, Crème Brûlée (CC) 24137; 1 ball each.

NEEDLES
US 5 (3.75mm) 16" circular and 2 DPNs, or size to obtain gauge

NOTIONS
Yarn Needle

GAUGE
22 sts and 28 rows = 4" in Herringbone Texture, blocked.

Notes:
The body of the dishcloth is worked, then stitches are picked up around and an applied icord is worked before adding a little loop hanger to finish.

Herringbone Texture
Row 1 (RS): [K2, p2] twice, k1, p2, k2, p2, k3, p2, k2, p2, k1, p2, k2, p2, k2.
Row 2 (WS): P1, *k2, p2, k2, p3, k2, p2, k2, p1; rep from * once more.
Row 3: K1, *p1, k2, p2, k5, p2, k2, p1, k1; rep from * once more.
Row 4: P3, k2, p2, k1, p1, k1, p2, k2., p5, k2, p2, k1, p1, k1, p2, k2, p3.
Rep these 4 rows for pattern.

DIRECTIONS
With circular needles and MC CO 39 sts.

Row 1 (WS): Purl.
Row 2 (RS): *K1, p1; rep from * to end.
Row 3: *K1, p1; rep from * to end.
Row 4: K1, p1, k1, work Herringbone Texture to last 3 sts, k1, p1, k1.

Work Row 4, completing 12 4-row Herringbone Texture repeats.

Next 2 Rows: *K1, p1; rep from * to end. K 1 row. BO all sts.

Finishing
Weave in ends, block to make a 7x7" square measured side to side, 9" diagonally across dishcloth.

Applied ICord
With circular needle and starting at your BO edge, pick up but do not knit 28 sts along each side of the square – 112 sts.

With CC, CO 2 sts on left needle. K3 – 2 CO sts and the first picked up stitch. Slide these stitches back to left hand needle. *K2, sl 1, k1, psso – 3 sts on right needle. Slip these stitches back to left hand needle. Rep from * until all picked up stitches are worked – 3 sts.

Swich to DPNs and work an icord for 2 ½". Cut yarn leaving a long tail and pull end through remaining stitches. Sew this end to the start of applied icord to attach, and put a little stitch at the top to join the bottom of your hanging loop. Weave in ends and block again to measurements.

BRICK-A-BRACK

by Beth Major

Learn how to manage your tension by creating a beautiful set of cloths. This easy crochet dishcloth uses two colors of Shine Worsted so you easily match your kitchen décor.

FINISHED MEASUREMENTS
Approximate 10" square

YARN
Knit Picks Shine Sport (60% Pima Cotton, 40% Modal; 110 yards/50g): Sweet Potato 26675 (color A), Serenade 24487 (color B); 1 ball each.

HOOKS
US G/6 (4mm)

NOTIONS
Yarn Needle

GAUGE
8 sts and 10 rows = 2" in SC (Gauge for this project is approximate)

Special Stitches
Deep V-SC
Insert hook into designated CH 1 sp, YO and pull up a loop even with your stitching (be careful to do this fairly loosely, too much tension with cause the stitches to pull up and squeeze together) YO and pull though both loops.

DIRECTIONS
Row 1: With color B, CH 44, SC in second CH from hook and in each CH across – 43 SC

Row 2: Switch to color A, CH 1, SC in next 6 SC, *CH 1, sk next SC, SC in next 5 SC* repeat from * to * across, SC in last 6 SC.

Row 3: CH 2, turn, HDC in each SC and CH 1-sp across.

Row 4: CH 1, SC in first HDC and in each HDC across.

Row 5: Switch to color B, CH 1, SC in first SC, *SC in next 5 SC , work Deep V-SC in CH 1-sp from a Row 2, Sk SC under the Deep V-SC, * repeat from * to * across, SC in last 6 SC.

Row 6: Switch to color A, CH 1, SC in first 3 SC, *CH 1, sk next SC, SC in next 5 SC* repeat from * to * across, SC in last 3 SC.

Row 7: Repeat Row 3

Row 8: Repeat Row 4

Row 9: Switch to color B, CH 1, SC in first 3 SC, work Deep V-SC into CH 1-sp from a Row 6, sk SC under deep V-SC, *SC in next 5 SC, work Deep V-SC into CH 1-sp from a Row 6, sk SC under deep V-SC * repeat from * to * across, SC in last 3 SC.

Repeat Rows 2-9 until piece measures approximately 10 inches square finish with either a Row 5 or a Row 9. Do not fasten off.

Edging
Continuing with color B, do not turn, *3 sc in corner, work 43 sc along edge of cloth* repeat for each edge, join to first sc with a SL ST, CH 1. Fasten off.

Finishing
Weave in ends.

PUMPKING

by Teresa Gregorio

This dishcloth tribute to the king of gourds features garter stitch with "outlines" of stockinette to create a reversible fabric that gives the look of a pumpkin from each side.

FINISHED MEASUREMENTS
Approximately 8x8" square

YARN
Knit Picks CotLin (70% Tanguis Cotton, 30% Linen; 123 yards/50g): MC: Clementine 24460, CC: Sprout 24462; 1 ball each.

NEEDLES
US 5 (3.75mm) straight or circular needles, or size to obtain gauge

NOTIONS
Yarn Needle

GAUGE
18 sts and 36 rows = 4" over garter patterns, blocked.

Notes:
Special abbreviations
KFBF (Knit Front Back Front)
Knit into front and back on next stitch, then knit in the front of the stitch again. 2 sts inc.

KFBFB (Knit Front Back Front Back)
Knit into the front and back of the next st, then knit into the front and back of the same st. 3 sts inc.

DIRECTIONS
Pumpkin
With MC, CO 5 sts.

Increasing
Row 1: KFBF, KFBF, KFBFB, KFBF, KFBF. (16 sts)
Row 2: Sl 1, *K2, P1* rep 4 more times.
Row 3: Sl 1, K to end.
Row 4: Repeat row 2.
Row 5: Sl 1, *KFB, KFB, K1* rep 4 more times. (26 sts)
Row 6: Sl 1, *K4, P1* rep 4 more times.
Row 7: Repeat row 3.
Row 8: Repeat row 6.
Row 9: Sl 1, *KFB, K2, KFB, K1* rep 4 more times. (36 sts)
Row 10: Sl 1, *K6, P1* rep 4 more times.
Row 11: Repeat row 3.
Row 12: Repeat row 10.
Row 13: Repeat row 3.
Row 14: Repeat row 10.
Row 15: Sl 1, K12, KFB, K1, KFB, K4, KFB, K1, KFB, K to end. (40 sts)
Row 16: Sl 1, K6, P1, K7, P1, K8, P1, K7, P1, K6, P1.
Row 17: Repeat row 3.
Row 18: Repeat row 16.

Repeat Rows 17 and 18 until piece is 6" long.

Decreasing
Row 1: Sl 1, K4, SSK, K6, SSK, K10, K2TOG, K6, K2TOG, K to end. (36 sts)
Row 2: Sl 1, K5, P1, K6, P1, K8, P1, K6, P1, K5, P1.
Row 3: Sl 1, K to end.
Row 4: Repeat row 2.
Row 5: Sl 1, K3, SSK, K5, SSK, K10, K2TOG, K5, K2TOG, K to end. (32 sts)
Row 6: Sl 1, K4, P1, K5, P1, K8, P1, K5, P1, K4, P1.
Row 7: Sl 1, K2, SSK, K4, SSK, K1, SSK, K4, K2TOG, K1, K2TOG, K4, K2TOG, K to end. (26 sts)
Row 8: Sl 1, K3, P1, K4, P1, K6, P1, K4, P1, K3, P1.
Row 9: Sl 1, SSSK, K1, SSK, SSK, K8, K2TOG, K2TOG, K1, K3TOG, K1. (18 sts)
Row 10: Sl 1, K1, P1, K2, P1, K6, P1, K2, P1, K1, P1.
Row 11: Sl 1, *SSK* repeat 3 more times, *K2TOG* repeat 3 more times, K1. (10 sts)
Row 12: Sl 1, P1, K1, P1, K2, P1, K1, P2.

Cut yarn.

Stem
Change to CC.
Row 13: Sl 1, K1, PSSO, P1, K1, K2TOG, K1, P1, SL 1, K1, PSSO. (7 sts)
Row 14: Sl 1, *K1, P1* repeat 2 more times.
Row 15: Sl 1, *P1, K1* repeat 2 more times.
Repeat rows 14 and 15 until Stem is 1" long.
BO in pattern.

Vine
With CC, CO 16 sts.
BO knit wise.

Finishing
Stitch Vine to Stem. Weave in ends, wash and block to diagram.

BELTED STRIPES

by The Knit Picks Design Team

Belted Stripes is a fun and visually interesting twist on the simple stripe pattern, making good use of a few slipped stitches. It can be made in two colors as shown in or in one color if a solid dishcloth is desired. The high relief textures makes for a very useful dishcloth.

FINISHED MEASUREMENTS
9.5" high x 8" wide

YARN
Knit Picks Dishie (100% cotton, 190 yds/100g): Color A (CA): Navy 26670; Color B (CB): Blue 25787; 1 ball each

NEEDLES
US 7 (4.5mm) straight or circular needles, or size to obtain gauge

NOTIONS
Yarn Needle

GAUGE
18 sts and 40 rows = 4" over Belted Stripes pattern, blocked. .

Notes:
Garter stitch
All rows: knit.

DIRECTIONS
With CB, CO 49 sts. Work 6 rows in garter stitch.

Belted Stripes Pattern
Row 1, and 3 (RS): With CA, knit.
Row 2 and 4: With CA, k2, purl to last 2 sts, k2.
Row 5 and 7: With CB, k2, P3, *sl3 WYIF, p9, rep from *, end last rep with p3, k2.
Row 6 and 8: With CB, k5, *sl3 WYIB, k9, rep from *, end last rep with k5.
Row 9, and 11: With CA, knit
Row 10, and 12: With CA, k2, purl to last 2 sts, k2.
Row 13 and 15: With CB, k2, P9, *sl3 WYIF, p9, rep from *, k2.
Row 14 and 16: With CB, k11, *sl3 WYIB, k9, rep from *, end last rep with k11.

Rep rows 1-16 another 3 times. Work rows 1-4 another time.

With CB, work 6 rows in garter stitch. BO.

Finishing
Weave in ends, wash and block gently.

SEPTEMBER

CELEBRATION

by Joyce Fassbender

It's time to celebrate! Turn any clean-up into a party with this cute washcloth. It is worked in the round from the center outward. The balloons are worked separately and then sewn on.

FINISHED MEASUREMENTS
10" diameter

YARN
Knit Picks Shine Sport (60% Pima Cotton, 40% Modal; 110 yards/50g): MC: Cream 23615, CC1: Iris 24789, CC2: White 24486; 1 ball each.

NEEDLES
US 2.5 (3.0mm) DPNs
US 4 (3.5mm) DPNs and 16 inch circular needles, or size to obtain gauge

NOTIONS
Yarn Needle

GAUGE
22 sts and 30 rows = 4" stockinette stitch.

Notes:

Pass 2 Slipped Stitches Over (p2sso): pass 2 slipped stitch over knitted stitch on right needle

Slip 2 (s2): slip 2 stitches together knitwise from left needle to right needle

Make bobble (MB): (K1 to the front, K1 to back of same stitch) twice, K1 to the front. Results in five stitches in one stitch. Turn work, P these five stitches. Turn work, K the five stitches. Turn work, P the five stitches. Turn work, starting with stitch five and working one stitch at a time, pass stitches five through two over stitch one.

I-cord
Using DPNs, K all stitches. *Without turning, slide stitches from the right to the left side of needle. K all stitches.* Repeat until desired length. To finish, cut yarn and run it through the remaining stitches. Pull to tighten.

Circular Cast On
Pinch the working yarn between the first and middle finger of your left hand so the end of the yarn comes out behind your fingers. Wrap the working yarn tail around the ring and pinky fingers of your left hand, holding the yarn tail firmly with your right hand. Point the tips of these fingers down toward your palm. *Using your right hand, insert the point of your needle (you can use double points or a circular) under the yarn across the back of your ring and pinky fingers (the 'first loop') from front to back. Pass the needle over the working yarn and draw a loop out from under the first loop; this creates one cast-on stitch. YO.* Repeat from * until you have cast on the required number of stitches. Note: If you need an even number of stitches, you will need to cast on the final stitch as a standard yarn over when you begin your first round of knitting. Arrange the stitches on your double point needles to begin knitting in the round.
Tug on the yarn tail to draw the stitches into a tighter circle.

DIRECTIONS
Dishcloth
Cast-on 8 stitches in MC using size 4 DPNs and a circular cast on. Place marker and join in the round taking care not to twist stitches. Knit one round.

Set Up Rows
Row 1: * K1, M1* eight times. 16 sts.
Row 2: K all stitches.

Work Body
Row 1: * K1, M1, K1, M1, PM,*eight times. 32 sts.
Row 2: K all stitches.
Row 3: K all stitches.
Row 4: K all stitches.
Row 5: * K1, M1, K to marker, M1, SM, *eight times.
Row 6: K all stitches.

Repeats rows 3-6 five more times. Switch from DPNs to circular needles as needed. 128 sts.

Work next row as: MB, m1, K1, *MB, K2* repeat * 42 times. (Total of 43 bobbles.) 129 sts.
Work one row as: K all stitches

Finishing:
Bind off loosely. Weave in ends, wash and block to finished measurements.

Balloons
Short string balloon (make 2)
With Size 4 DPNs, cast on 5 stitches in CC1 using long tail cast-on. P one row.
Row 1: K1, M1, K3, M1, K1. 7 sts.
Row 2 and all even rows: P all stitches.
Row 3: K1, M1, K5, M1, K1. 9 sts.
Row 5: K all stitches.
Row 7: K1, k2tog, K3, ssk, K1. 7 sts.
Row 9: K1, k2tog, K1, ssk, K1. 5 sts.
Row 11: K1, s2, K1, p2sso, K1. 3 sts.
Switch to CC2 and size 2.5 DPNs. Work three inches of i-cord.

Long string balloon (make 1)
With Size 4 DPNs, cast on 5 stitches in CC1 using long tail cast-on. P one row.
Row 1: K1, M1, K3, M1, K1. 7 sts.
Row 2 and all even rows: P all stitches.
Row 3: K1, M1, K5, M1, K1. 9 sts.
Row 5: K all stitches.
Row 7: K1, ssk, K3, k2tog, K1. 7 sts.
Row 9: K1, ssk, K1, k2tog, K1. 5 sts.
Row 11: K1, s2, K1, p2sso, K1. 3 sts.
Switch to CC2 and size 2.5 DPNs. Work six inches of i-cord.

Finishing
Weave in ends. Tie i-cord of long string balloon around other balloon strings. Sew balloons to body of dish cloth.

RIPPLES

by The Knit Picks Design Team

Ripples is a fun textured dishcloth worked with knits and purls. It is very easy and is a good choice for beginner knitters. The chevron pattern moves up and down the dishcloth like rippling waves on a beach.

FINISHED MEASUREMENTS
9x9"

YARN
Knit Picks Dishie (worsted weight, 100% cotton, 190 yds/100g): Azure 25412, 1 ball

NEEDLES
US 7 (4.5mm) straight or circular needles, or size to obtain gauge

NOTIONS
Yarn Needle

GAUGE
18 sts and 26 rows = 4" over pattern, blocked. .

Notes:
Garter stitch
All rows: knit.

DIRECTIONS
CO 39 sts. Work 8 rows in garter stitch

Row 1 (RS): k7, *p1, k7, rep from *.
Row 2: k3, p3, *k3, p5, rep from *, end k3, p3, k3.
Row 3: k5, *p2, k1, p2, k3, rep from *, end p2, k1, p2, k5.
Row 4: k3, p1, *k2, p3, k2, p1, rep from *, k3.
Row 5: k4, *p1, k5, p1, k1, rep from *, k3.
Row 6: k3, purl to last 3 sts, k3.

Rep rows 1-6 another 7 times.

Work 8 rows in garter stitch. BO all sts.

Finishing
Weave in ends, wash and block gently.

SLIPPED STRIPES

by Faith Schmidt

Slipped Stripes is a fun and easy knit. The stitch pattern is easy to memorize, and, while not reversible, looks great on both sides. It can easily be resized to fit your needs, and would make a thoughtful hostess gift.

FINISHED MEASUREMENTS
Approx. 10.75" square

YARN
Knit Picks Dishie (100% Cotton; 190 yards/100g): Begonia 25790; 1 ball

NEEDLES
US 6 (4.5mm) straight or circular needles, or size to obtain gauge

NOTIONS
Yarn Needle

GAUGE
19.5 sts = 4" over Stockinette Stitch, unblocked. Exact gauge is not important to this project.

Notes:
To resize, cast on a multiple of 3+2, and knit to desired length.

Slipped Stitch Pattern (worked flat)
Row 1 (RS): P2, *sl 1 knitwise wyib, p2, repeat from * to end of row
Row 2 : K2, *sl 1 purlwise wyif, k2, repeat from * to end of row
Row 3: Knit
Row 4: Purl

DIRECTIONS
CO 50 sts using the Long Tail Cast-on.

Work in Slipped Stitch Pattern until piece measures approx. 10.75", or is square, ending with a Row 2.

BO in purl.

Finishing
Weave in ends, block if desired.

NICE-N-EASY

by Beth Major

Create a quick and easy cloth for the spa or for the kitchen! This pattern will become your go-to for a last minute gift.

FINISHED MEASUREMENTS
10" Square, approximately

YARN
Knit Picks Shine Sport (60% Pima Cotton, 40% Modal; 110 yards/50g): Hydrangea 23813; 1 ball.

HOOKS
US G/6 (4mm)

NOTIONS
Yarn Needle

GAUGE
9 sts and 10 rows = 2" in SC

Notes:

Reverse SC (or Crab Stitch) - RSC
Working left to right, insert hook into next stitch, YO and pull up a loop, YO and pull through both loops on hook.

DIRECTIONS
Row 1: CH 43
Row 2: CH 1, turn, SC in each CH across – 42 sts
Row 3: CH 1, turn, SC in BLO of each SC across – 42 sts

Repeat Row 3 until cloth measures 10 inches, do not fasten off.

Edging
Row 1: CH 1, do not turn, work 3 SC into last SC, (evenly space 42 SC along edge of cloth, 3 SC in next corner) 3 times, SC in each sc across, join with SL ST.

Row 2: CH 1, do not turn, work RSC in each SC around, join with SL ST to first ST. Fasten off.

Finishing
Weave in ends, wash and block.

OCTOBER

RADIO WAVE

by The Knit Picks Design Team

Radio Wave features textured diamonds worked with slipped stitches and surrounded by a garter stitch border. The high relief textures makes for a very useful dishcloth.

FINISHED MEASUREMENTS
9.5" wide x 8.5" high

YARN
Knit Picks Dishie (100% cotton, 190 yds/100g): Aster 25413; 1 ball

NEEDLES
US 7 (4.5mm) straight or circular needles, or size to obtain gauge

NOTIONS
Yarn Needle

GAUGE
18 sts and 26 rows = 4" over pattern, blocked. .

Notes:
Garter stitch
All rows: knit.

DIRECTIONS
CO 43 sts. Work 8 rows in garter stitch

Set up row: k2, p to last 2 sts, k2.

Row 1, 3 and 5 (WS): knit.
Row 2 and 4: k2, p to last 2 sts, k2.
Row 6: k2, p3, *drop next st off needle and unravel 5 rows down; then insert right-hand needle into the st from behind, lift the st and the 5 loose strands above it onto left-hand needle, and purl the st and the 5 loose strands all together, p3, rep from *, k2.
Row 7, 9 and 11: knit.
Row 8 and 10: k2, p to last 2 sts, k2.
Row 12: k2, p1, *drop next st off needle and unravel 5 rows down; then insert right-hand needle into the st from behind, lift the st and the 5 loose strands above it onto left-hand needle, and purl the st and the 5 loose strands all together, p3, rep from *, end last repeat with p1 instead of p3, k2.

Rep rows 1-12 another 4 times.

Work 8 rows in garter stitch. BO all sts.

Finishing
Weave in ends, wash and block gently.

MUIDERSLOT

by Allyson Dykhuizen

Castle Muiderslot is a big castle in Amsterdam surrounded by a moat, much like this dishcloth's checkerboard body is surrounded by applied icord. A stretch? For sure. But this Dutch girl just had to pay a very tiny tribute to her family's homeland, so why not in the form of a dishcloth?

FINISHED MEASUREMENTS
7.5" square measured side to side, 9.5" measured diagonally, 1 ¼" hanging loop.

YARN
Knit Picks CotLin (70% Tanguis Cotton, 30% Linen; 123 yards/50g):): Gosling (MC) 26239, Lichen (CC) 26674; 1 ball each.

NEEDLES
US 5 (3.75mm) 16" circular and 2 DPNs, or size to obtain gauge

NOTIONS
Yarn Needle
Small Crochet Hook

GAUGE
22 sts and 28 rows = 4" in Plaid Pattern, blocked.

Notes:
The body of the dishcloth is worked, then stitches are picked up around and an applied icord is worked before adding a little loop hanger to finish.

Completing Vertical Plaid Columns:
With CC held on WS and beginning at top of first purl column, insert crochet hook from RS into first st of purl column and pull up a loop of yarn from underneath. *Leaving loop on hook, insert hook from RS into next st of purl column and pull up a loop from underneath, pull this second loop through first loop, rep from * to last purl st, cut yarn and pull tail through last loop. Insert hook through last loop from WS and pull yarn tail to WS.

DIRECTIONS
With circular needles and MC CO 37 sts.

Rows 1 and 3 (RS): K4, *p1, k4; rep from * to last 3 sts, p1, k2.
Rows 2 and 4 (WS): P2, *k1, p4; rep from * to last 5 sts, k1, p4. Cut MC after Row 4.
Rows 5 and 7: With CC work as for Row 1.
Rows 6 and 8: With CC work as for Row 2.

Work rows 1-8 6 times total, then rows 1-3 once more. BO all Sts. Complete Vertical Plaid Columns as described in Notes.

Finishing
Weave in ends, block to make a 7x7" square measured side to side, 9" diagonally across dishcloth.

Applied ICord
With circular needle and starting at your BO edge, pick up but do not knit 28 sts along each side of the square – 112 sts.

With CC, CO 2 sts on left needle. K3 – 2 CO sts and the first picked up stitch. Slide these stitches back to left hand needle. *K2, sl 1, k1, psso – 3 sts on right needle. Slip these stitches back to left hand needle. Rep from * until all picked up stitches are worked – 3 sts.

Swich to DPNs and work an icord for 2 ½". Cut yarn leaving a long tail and pull end through remaining stitches. Sew this end to the start of applied icord to attach, and put a little stitch at the top to join the bottom of your hanging loop. Weave in ends and block again to measurements.

SUMMER LINES

by Gillian Grimm

This bias knit dishcloth features fine contrasting lines reminiscent of mattress ticking and striped summer awnings. The bias garter stitch creates a soft but nubby surface for scrubbing away at those dishes!

FINISHED MEASUREMENTS
6" long x 6" wide.

YARN
Knit Picks Dishie Yarn (100% Cotton 190 yards/100 grams)
MC: Linen 25400, CC: Navy 26670; 1 skein each

NEEDLES
US 7 (3.75 mm) circular needles

NOTIONS
Yarn Needle

GAUGE
20 sts and 28 rows = 4 inches in bias garter stitch

Bias Stitch Increase Pattern (worked flat)
Row 1: (WS) Knit
Row 2: (RS) K1,M1R, K till 1 st rem, M1L, K1. (2 sts. inc.)

Bias Stitch Decrease Pattern (worked flat)
Row 1: Knit
Row 2: K2tog, K til 2 sts rem. SSK (2 sts. dec.)

DIRECTIONS
With MC, CO 1 sts.
Row 1 (WS): K1
Row 2: (RS): Using the backward loop method, CO1, K1, CO1. (3 sts)
Row 3: Knit
Row 4: K1,M1R, K till 1 st rem, M1L, K1. (5 sts) Place marker on this side to denote increase side of the work.

*Work Bias Stitch Increase Pattern in MC two more times. Switch to CC and work Bias Stitch Increase Pattern one time. * Repeat between *'s 5 more times. (41 sts)

Switch to MC and begin decreases.
*Row 1 (WS): Knit
Row 2 (RS): K2tog, K till 2 remain, SSK (2 sts decreased)

Repeat Bias Stitch Decrease Pattern once more in MC. Switch to CC and work Bias Stitch Decrease Pattern once in CC.*

Repeat between *'s Until 5 sts remain. Continue with Bias Stitch Decrease pattern in MC until 3 sts remain. Sl 1, K2tog, PSSO. Break yarn and pull through.

Finishing
Weave in ends, wash and block to dimensions.

ACE OF SPADES

by Stana D. Sortor

This Ace of Spades washcloth has double moss stitch pattern. Start with the stem, then work the first part of the leaf, and the second part of leaf, carefully joining all three pieces together.

FINISHED MEASUREMENTS
8.5" wide, flat x 9.5" high

YARN
Knit Picks Shine Worsted (60% Pima Cotton, 40% Modal; 75 yards/50g): Black 25348, 1 ball.

NEEDLES
US 6 (4.25mm) straight or circular needles, or size to obtain gauge

NOTIONS
Yarn Needle
Stitch Holder

GAUGE
18 sts and 30 rows = 4" in Double Moss Stitch pattern, blocked.

DIRECTIONS

Stem:
CO 6 sts.
Row 1: K2, P2, K2 (6 sts total)
Row 2: P2, K2, P2.
Row 3: P2tog, K2, P2tog (4 sts total)
Row 4: K1, P2, K1.
Row 5: P2tog, P2tog (2 sts total)
Row 6: K2.
Row 7: P2.
Row 8: K2.

Cut yarn, leave on a stitch holder or scrape yarn.

Leaf Part 1:
CO 10 sts.
Row 1: (K2, P2) 2x, K2 (10 sts total)
Row 2: (P2, K2) 2x, P2.
Row 3: KFB, P1, K2, P2, K2, P1, KFB (12 sts total)
Row 4: P1, (K2, P2) 2x, K2, P1.
Row 5: KFB, (K2, P2) 2x, K2, KFB (14 sts total)
Row 6: (K2, P2) 3x, K2.

Cut yarn, leave on a stitch holder or scrape yarn.

Leaf Part 2:
CO 10 sts.
Row 1: (K2, P2) 2x, K2 (10 sts total)
Row 2: (P2, K2) 2x, P2.
Row 3: KFB, P1, K2, P2, K2, P1, KFB (12 sts total)
Row 4: P1, (K2, P2) 2x, K2, P1.
Row 5: KFB, (K2, P2) 2x, K2, KFB (14 sts total)
Row 6: (K2, P2) 3x, K2.

Carefully transfer the first part of the leaf, then the stem, then the second part of the leaf on the same needle. Continue across all three pieces joining them together.

Row 7: (K2, P2) 7x, K2 (30 sts total)
Row 8: (P2, K2) 7x, P2.
Row 9: KFB, P1, (K2, P2) 6x, K2, P1, KFB (32 sts total)
Row 10: P1, (K2, P2) 7x, K2, P1.
Row 11: P1, (K2, P2) 7x, K2, P1.
Row 12: K1, (P2, K2) 7x, P2, K1.
Row 13: KFB, P2, (K2, P2) 7x, KFB (34 sts total)
Row 14: (P2, K2) 8x, P2.

Row 15: (P2, K2) 8x, P2.
Row 16: (K2, P2) 8x, K2.
Row 17: KFB, K1, (P2, K2) 7x, P2, K1, KFB (36 sts total)
Row 18: K1, (P2, K2) 8x, P2, K1.
Row 19: K1, (P2, K2) 8x, P2, K1.
Row 20: P1, (K2, P2) 8x, K2, P1.
Row 21: KFB, (K2, P2) 8x, K2, KFB (38 sts total)
Row 22: (K2, P2) 9x, K2.
Row 23: (K2, P2) 9x, K2.
Row 24: (P2, K2) 9x, P2.
Row 25: (P2, K2) 9x, P2.
Row 26: (K2, P2) 9x, K2.
Row 27: KFB, K1, (P2, K2) 8x, P2, K1, KFB (40 sts total)
Row 28: K1, (P2, K2) 9x, P2, K1.
Row 29: K1, (P2, K2) 9x, P2, K1.
Row 30: P1, (K2, P2) 9x, K2, P1.

Row 31: P1, (K2, P2) 9x, K2, P1.
Row 32: K1, (P2, K2) 9x, P2, K1.
Row 33: SSK, P1, (K2, P2) 8x, K2, P1, K2tog (38 sts total)
Row 34: (K2, P2) 9x, K2.
Row 35: SSK, (P2, K2) 8x, P2, K2tog (36 sts total)
Row 36: P1, (K2, P2) 8x, K2, P1.
Row 37: SSK, K1, (P2, K2) 7x, P2, K1, K2tog (34 sts total)
Row 38: (P2, K2) 8x, P2.
Row 39: SSK, (K2, P2) 7x, K2, K2tog (32 sts total)
Row 40: K1, (P2, K2) 7x, P2, K1.

Row 41: SSK, P1, (K2, P2) 6x, K2, P1, K2tog (30 sts total)
Row 42: (K2, P2) 7x, K2.
Row 43: SSK, (P2, K2) 6x, P2, K2tog (28 sts total)
Row 44: P1, (K2, P2) 6x, K2, P1.
Row 45: SSK, K1, (P2, K2) 5x, P2, K1, K2tog (26 sts total)
Row 46: (P2, K2) 6x, P2.
Row 47: SSK, (K2, P2) 5x, K2, K2tog (24 sts total)
Row 48: K1, (P2, K2) 5x, P2, K1.
Row 49: SSK, P1, (K2, P2) 4x, K2, P1, K2tog. (22 sts total)
Row 50: (K2, P2) 5x, K2.
Row 51: SSK, (P2, K2) 4x, P2, K2tog. (20 sts total)
Row 52: P1, (K2, P2) 4x, K2, P1.
Row 53: SSK, K1, (P2, K2) 3x, P2, K1, K2tog (18 sts total)

Row 54: (P2, K2) 4x, P2.
Row 55: SSK, (K2, P2) 3x, K2, K2tog (16 sts total)
Row 56: K1, (P2, K2) 3x, P2, K1.
Row 57: SSK, P1, (K2, P2) 2x, K2, P1, K2tog (14 sts total)
Row 58: (K2, P2) 3x, K2.
Row 59: SSK, (P2, K2) 2x, P2, K2tog (12 sts total)
Row 60: P1, (K2, P2) 2x, K2, P1.

Row 61: SSK, K1, P2, K2, P2, K1, K2tog (10 sts total)
Row 62: (P2, K2) 2x, P2.
Row 63: SSK, K2, P2, K2, K2tog (8 sts total)
Row 64: K1, P2, K2, P2, K1.
Row 65: SSK, P1, K2, P1, K2tog (6 sts total)
Row 66: K2, P2, K2.
Row 67: SSK, P2, K2tog (4 sts total)
Row 68: P1, K2, P1.
Row 69: SSK, K2tog. (2 sts total)
Row 70: P2.

Row 71: Bind off.

Finishing
Weave in ends, wash and block to finished measurements

BIG ZIG

by Kendra Nitta

This boldly zig-zagged dishcloth knits up quickly and makes a great teacher gift or stocking stuffer.

FINISHED MEASUREMENTS
9" square

YARN
Knit Picks CotLin (70% Tanguis Cotton, 30% Linen; 123 yards/50g): Cerise 24835, 1 ball

NEEDLES
US 5 (3.75mm) straight or circular needles or size to obtain gauge

NOTIONS
Yarn Needle
Stitch Markers

GAUGE
24 sts and 34 rows = 4" in St st, blocked. (Gauge for this project is approximate).

DIRECTIONS
CO 54 sts. Work Rows 1-77 from Big Zig chart.

BO all sts.

Finishing
Weave in ends, wash and block to finished dimensions.

Big Zig Chart

Legend

knit
☐ RS: knit stitch
WS: purl stitch

purl
● RS: purl stitch
WS: knit stitch

Big Zig

SUNNY DAYS

by The Knit Picks Design Team

Sunny Days is an easy and elegant lace dishcloth. It knits up quickly and looks stunning, the perfect choice for a stylish kitchen.

FINISHED MEASUREMENTS
9" wide x 8" high

YARN
Knit Picks Dishie (100% cotton, 190 yds/100g): Azure 25412; 1 ball

NEEDLES
US 7 (4.5mm) straight or circular needles, or size to obtain gauge

NOTIONS
Yarn Needle

GAUGE
18 sts and 26 rows = 4" over pattern, blocked. .

Notes:
Garter stitch
All rows: knit.

DIRECTIONS
CO 40 sts. Work 12 rows of garter stitch.

Row 1 (RS): k2, *k3, pass 1st of last 3 sts over last k2, k3*; rep from *, k2.
Row 2: k2, *p4, yo, p1*; rep from *, k2
Row 3: k2, *k3, k3, pass 1st of last 3 sts over last k2*; rep from *, k2.
Row 4: k2, *p1, yo, p4*; rep from *, k2.

Repeat rows 1-4 another 9 times.

Work 12 rows in garter stitch. BO all sts.

Finishing
Weave in ends, wash and block gently.

HEIRLOOM LINEN

by Kalurah Hudson

Heirloom Linen is crocheted in a pretty linen stitch, mimicking the look of timeless linen cloth. Delicate picots and shells trim the edges of the dishcloth, lending to the vintage feel. The dishcloth and edging are both charted.

FINISHED MEASUREMENTS
7" wide x 22.5", including edging

YARN
Knit Picks CotLin (70% Tanguis Cotton, 30% Linen; 123 yards/50g): Gosling 26239, 2 balls.
Knit Picks Shine Sport (60% Pima Cotton, 40% Modal® natural beech wood fiber; 110 yards/50g): Cream 23615, 1 ball.

HOOKS
US G (4.25mm) crochet hook, or size to obtain gauge and US E (3.50mm) crochet hook, or a hook 1 size smaller than gauge

NOTIONS
Tapestry Needle

GAUGE
Using G hook and CotLin: 11 sts and 20 rows = 4" in Linen stitch, blocked. (1sc+ch1 counts as 1 stitch)

Notes:
The smaller hook size is used to work the first and last rows of the dishcloth and also for the edging. The larger hook is only used when working the linen stitch.

3dcdec - 3 Double Crochet Decrease
Yo, insert hook into st, pull up a loop, yo and pull through 2 loops on hook, *yo, insert hook into the same st, pull up a loop, yo and pull through 2 loops on hook* 2 times, yo and pull through rem 3 st on hook. (1 3dcdec complete)

Picot
Ch3, sl st in 1st chain to close. (1 picot complete)

Flsc - Front Loop Single Crochet
Work a single crochet stitch into the front loop only.

DIRECTIONS
Dishcloth
Start with smaller hook and CotLin.

Ch. 41.

Row 1: 1sc in second ch from hook, 1sc in ea ch to end. (40sc)

Switch to larger hook.

Row 2: Ch2, turn. Sk first sc, 1sc in nx sc, *ch1, sk nx sc, 1sc in nx sc* rep to last sc.

Row 3: Ch2, turn. Sk first sc, 1sc in nx ch1-sp, *ch1, sk nx sc, 1sc in nx ch1-sp* rep to end, work last sc in the ch2-sp.

Row 4: Ch2, turn. Sk first sc, 1sc in nx ch1-sp, *ch1, sk nx sc, 1sc in nx ch1-sp* rep to end, work last sc in the ch2-sp.

Rows 5-92: Rep rows 3 & 4.

Switch back to smaller hook.

Row 93: Ch 1, turn. 1sc in first sc, *1sc in ch1-sp, 1sc in nx sc* rep to end, work last sc in ch2-sp. Tie off.

Edging
Using smaller hook and Shine Sport. Join yarn to the first single crochet of the dishcloth, with RS facing you.

Row 1: Ch1, (does not count as first st). Do not turn. 1sc in ea sc to end. (40sc)

Row 2: Ch1, (does not count as a st) turn. 1flsc in ea sc to end. (40flsc)

Row 3: Ch2, (does not count as a st) turn. Sk first 3 flsc, 3dcdec into nx st, make picot, ch1, 3dcdec in same st, make picot, ch1, 3dcdec in same st, *make picot, ch2, sk nx 4 flsc, 1sc in nx flsc, make a picot, sc in the nx sc, ch2, sk nx 4 flsc, 3dcdec into nx st, make picot, ch1, 3dcdec in same st, make picot, ch1, 3dcdec in same st, * rep 2 more times to fourth st from the end, make picot, ch2, sk nx 2 flsc, sl st in last flsc. Tie off.

Rotate dischcloth to bottom edge, with RS facing you join yarn to the first ch of foundation ch. Rep rows 1-3 of edging instructions.

Finishing
Weave in all ends and wet block to finished dimensions.

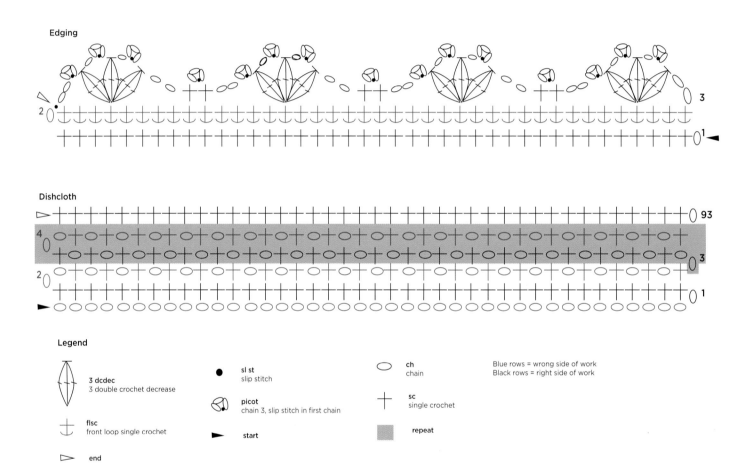

TOPAZ FACECLOTH

by Joyce Fassbender

This pretty facecloth uses simple knit and purl stitches to create a beautiful texture. Surrounded by a seed stitch border, this is a pattern you'll turn to again and again.

FINISHED MEASUREMENTS
8" wide x 8" high

YARN
Knit Picks CotLin (70% Tanguis Cotton, 30% Linen; 123 yards/50g): Clementine, 24460; 1 ball

NEEDLES
US 6 (4.0mm) straight or circular needles, or size to obtain gauge

NOTIONS
Yarn Needle

GAUGE
24 sts and 28 rows = 4" stockinette stitch.

Notes: The cloth is charted with a textured center surrounded by a seed stitch edge.

Boxed stitch pattern repeat is worked three times across rows.

DIRECTIONS
CO 47 stitches using long tail cast on.

Set up rows:

Rows 1 – 5: *K1, P1* , rep between ** across row, K1

Row 6: [K1, P1] two times, K until last 4 sts, [P1, K1] two times

Work Chart

Work rows 1-10 of chart 1 five (5) times.

End rows:

Rows 1 – 5: *K1, P1* , rep between ** across row, K1

BO all sts..

Finishing
Weave in ends, wash, and block to size.

Topaz Chart

Legend

knit
RS: knit stitch
WS: purl stitch

purl
RS: purl stitch
WS: knit stitch

Pattern Repeat

BLACK DIAMOND

by Stana D. Sortor

Conquer your fears, and knit a black diamond dishcloth in seed stitch for all the skiing enthusiasts in your life. The last stitch at every row is slipped for a nicer edge, increases and decreases are done on the first and second to last stitches of rows.

FINISHED MEASUREMENTS
8.5" wide, x 9.5" high

YARN
Knit Picks Shine Worsted (60% Pima Cotton, 40% Modal; 75 yards/50g): Black 25348, 1 ball.

NEEDLES
US 6 (4mm) straight or circular needles, or size to obtain gauge

NOTIONS
Yarn Needle

GAUGE
18 sts and 30 rows = 4" in Seed Stitch pattern, blocked.

DIRECTIONS
CO 2 sts.

Row 1: KFB, KFB (4 sts total).
Row 2: P1, K1, P1, Sl. st.
Row 3: K1, KFB, KFB, Sl. st. (6 sts total).
Row 4: (P1, K1) 2x, P1, Sl. st.
Row 5: KFB, P1, K1, P1, KFB, Sl. st. (8 sts total).
Row 6: K1, (P1, K1) 3x, Sl. st.
Row 7: KFB, (K1, P1) 2x, K1, KFB, Sl. st. (10 sts total).
Row 8: (P1, K1) 4x, P1, Sl. st.
Row 9: KFB, P1, (K1, P1) 3x, KFB, Sl. st. (12 sts total).
Row 10: K1, (P1, K1) 5x, Sl. st.

Row 11: KFB, (K1, P1) 4x, K1, KFB, Sl. st. (14 sts total).
Row 12: (P1, K1) 6x, P1, Sl. st.
Row 13: KFB, P1, (K1, P1) 5x, KFB, Sl. st. (16 sts total).
Row 14: K1, (P1, K1) 7x, Sl. st.
Row 15: KFB, (K1, P1) 6x, K1, KFB, Sl. st. (18 sts total).
Row 16: (P1, K1) 8x, P1, Sl. st.
Row 17: KFB, P1, (K1, P1) 7x, KFB, Sl. st. (20 sts total).
Row 18: K1, (P1, K1) 9x, Sl. st.
Row 19: KFB, (K1, P1) 8x, K1, KFB, Sl. st. (22 sts total).
Row 20: (P1, K1) 10x, P1, Sl. st.

Row 21: KFB, P1, (K1, P1) 9x, KFB, Sl. st. (24 sts total).
Row 22: K1, (P1, K1) 11x, Sl. st.
Row 23: KFB, (K1, P1) 10x, K1, KFB, Sl. st. (26 sts total).
Row 24: (P1, K1) 12x, P1, Sl. st.
Row 25: KFB, P1, (K1, P1)11x, KFB, Sl. st. (28 sts total).
Row 26: K1, (P1, K1) 13x, Sl. st.
Row 27: KFB, (K1, P1) 12x, K1, KFB, Sl. st. (30 sts total).
Row 28: (P1, K1) 14x, P1, Sl. st.
Row 29: KFB, P1, (K1, P1) 13x, KFB, Sl. st. (32 sts total).
Row 30: K1, (P1, K1) 15x, Sl. st.

Row 31: KFB, (K1, P1) 14x, K1, KFB, Sl. st. (34 sts total).
Row 32: (P1, K1) 16x, P1, Sl. st.
Row 33: KFB, P1, (K1, P1) 15x, KFB, Sl. st. (36 sts total).
Row 34: K1, (P1, K1) 17x, Sl. st.
Row 35: KFB, (K1, P1) 16x, K1, KFB, Sl. st. (38 sts total).
Row 36: (P1, K1) 18x, P1, Sl. st.
Row 37: KFB, P1, (K1, P1) 17x, KFB, Sl. st. (40 sts total).
Row 38: K1, (P1, K1) 19x, Sl. st.
Row 39: SSK, P1, (K1, P1) 17x, K2tog, Sl. st. (38 sts total).
Row 40: (P1, K1) 18x, P1, Sl. st.

Row 41: SSK, (K1, P1) 16x, K1, K2tog, Sl. st. (36 sts total).
Row 42: K1, (P1, K1) 17x, Sl. st.
Row 43: SSK, P1, (K1, P1) 15x, K2tog, Sl. st. (34 sts total).
Row 44: (P1, K1) 16x, P1, Sl. st.
Row 45: SSK, (K1, P1) 14x, K1, K2tog, Sl. st. (32 sts total).
Row 46: K1, (P1, K1) 15x, Sl. St.
Row 47: SSK, P1, (K1, P1) 13x, K2tog, Sl. st. (30 sts total).
Row 48: (P1, K1) 14x, P1, Sl. st.
Row 49: SSK, (K1, P1) 12x, K1, K2tog, Sl. st. (28 sts total).
Row 50: K1, (P1, K1) 13x, Sl. st.

Row 51: SSK, P1 (K1, P1) 11x, K2tog, Sl. st. (26 sts total).
Row 52: (P1, K1) 12x, P1, Sl. st.
Row 53: SSK, (K1, P1) 10x, K1, K2tog, Sl. st. (24 sts total).
Row 54: K1, (P1, K1) 11x, Sl. st.
Row 55: SSK, P1 (K1, P1) 9x, K2tog, Sl. st. (22 sts total).
Row 56: (P1, K1) 10x, P1, Sl. st.
Row 57: SSK, (K1, P1) 8x, K1, K2tog, Sl. st. (20 sts total).
Row 58: K1, (P1, K1) 9x, Sl. st.
Row 59: SSK, P1 (K1, P1) 7x, K2tog, Sl. st. (18 sts total).
Row 60: (P1, K1) 8x, P1, Sl. st.

Row 61: SSK, (K1, P1) 6x, K1, K2tog, Sl. st. (16 sts total).
Row 62: K1, (P1, K1) 7x, Sl. st.
Row 63: SSK, P1, (K1, P1) 5x, K2tog, Sl. st. (14 sts total).
Row 64: (P1, K1) 6x, P1, Sl. st.
Row 65: SSK, (K1, P1) 4x, K1, K2tog, Sl. st. (12 sts total).
Row 66: K1, (P1, K1) 5x, Sl. st.
Row 67: SSK, P1, (K1, P1) 3x, K2tog, Sl. st. (10 sts total).
Row 68: (P1, K1) 4x, P1, Sl. st.
Row 69: SSK, (K1, P1) 2x, K1, K2tog, Sl. st. (8 sts total).
Row 70: K1, (P1, K1) 3x, Sl. st.

Row 71: SSK, P1, K1, P1, K2tog, Sl. st. (6 sts total).
Row 72: (P1, K1) 2x, P1, Sl. st.
Row 73: SSK, K1, K2tog, Sl. st. (4 sts total).
Row 74: K1, P1, K1, Sl. st.
Row 75: SSK, K2tog (2 sts total).
Row 76: Bind off.

Finishing
Weave in ends, wash and block to finished measurements

HOUSE OF CLUBS

by Stana D. Sortor

The last suit to create a dishcloth version of a deck of cards. This black club washcloth starts with the stem, then works the first and second parts of the leaves, and ends by carefully joining all three pieces together.

FINISHED MEASUREMENTS
8.5" wide, x 9.5" high

YARN
Knit Picks Shine Worsted (60% Pima Cotton, 40% Modal; 75 yards/50g): Black 25348; 1 ball.

NEEDLES
US 6 (4mm) straight or circular needles, or size to obtain gauge

NOTIONS
Yarn Needle
Stitch Holder or Scrap Yarn

GAUGE
18 sts and 30 rows = 4" in Knit pattern, blocked.

DIRECTIONS

Stem:
CO 8 sts.
Rows 1 - 2: K8.
Row 3: SSK, K4, K2tog (6 sts total).
Row 4: K6.
Row 5: SSK, K2, K2tog (4 sts total).
Row 6: K4.
Row 7: SSK, K2tog (2 sts total).
Rows 8 - 10: K2.
Cut yarn, leave on a stitch holder or scrap yarn.

Leaf Part 1
CO 10 sts.
Rows 1 - 2: K10.
Row 3: KFB, K8, KFB (12 sts total).
Row 4: K 12.
Row 5: KFB, K10, KFB (14 sts total).
Row 6: K14.
Cut yarn, leave on a stitch holder or scrap yarn.

Leaf Part 2
CO 10 sts.
Rows 1 - 2: K10
Row 3: KFB, K8, KFB (12 sts total)
Row 4: K 12
Row 5: KFB, K10, KFB (14 sts total)
Row 6: K14.
Carefully transfer the first part of the leaf, then the stem, then the second part of the leaf on the same needle. Continue across all three pieces joining them together.

Body
Rows 7 - 8: K30
Row 9: KFB, K28, KFB (32 sts total)
Rows 10 - 12: K32
Row 13: KFB, K30, KFB (34 sts total)
Rows 14 - 16: K34
Row 17: KFB, K32, KFB (36 sts total)
Rows 18 - 20: K36
Row 21: KFB, K34, KFB (38 sts total)
Rows 22 - 26: K38
Row 27: KFB, K36, KFB (40 sts total)
Rows 28 - 32: K40
Row 33: SSK, K34, K2tog (38 sts total)
Rows 34 - 36: K38
Row 37: SSK, K32, K2tog (36 sts total)
Rows 38 - 40: K36

At this point you will work with first 14 sts and leave the last 22 sts to work with later.
Row 41: SSK, K10, K2tog (12 sts total)
Row 42: K12
Row 43: SSK, K8, K2tog (10 sts total)
Row 44: K10
Row 45: Bind off.

Leave the middle 8 sts on a scrap yarn, reattach the yarn to the last 14 sts and repeat:
Row 41: SSK, K10, K2tog (12 sts total)
Row 42: K12
Row 43: SSK, K8, K2tog (10 sts total)
Row 44: K10
Row 45: Bind off.

Reattach the yarn to reminding 8 stitches and work as follow:
Rows 41 - 42: K8
Row 43: KFB, K6, KFB (10 sts total)
Row 44: K10
Row 45: KFB, K8, KFB (12 sts total)
Row 46: K12
Row 47: KFB, K10, KFB (14 sts total)
Row 48: K14
Row 49: KFB, K12, KFB (16 sts total)
Row 50: K16
Row 51: KFB, K14, KFB (18 sts total)
Row 52: K18
Row 53: KFB, K16, KFB (20 sts total)
Rows 54 - 58: K20
Row 59: SSK, K16, K2tog (18 sts total)
Rows 60 - 62: K18
Row 63: SSK, K14, K2tog. (16 sts total)
Row 64: K16
Row 65: SSK, K12, K2tog. (14 sts total)
Row 66: K14
Row 67: SSK, K10, K2tog (12 sts total)
Row 68: K12
Row 69: SSK, K8, K2tog (10 sts total)
Row 70: K10
Row 71: Bind off.

Finishing
Weave in ends, wash and block to finished measurements.

DECEMBER

SEAWEED

by The Knit Picks Design Team

Seaweed is a fun textured pattern worked with knits and purls that resembles kelp waving gently to and fro. A simple garter stitch border finishes off this gorgeous dishcloth.

FINISHED MEASUREMENTS
9x9"

YARN
Knit Picks Dishie (100% cotton, 190 yds/100g): Honeydew 25410; 1 ball

NEEDLES
US 7 (4.5mm) straight or circular needles, or size to obtain gauge

NOTIONS
Yarn Needle

GAUGE
18 sts and 26 rows = 4" over pattern, blocked. .

Notes:
Garter stitch
All rows: knit.

DIRECTIONS
Cast on 44 sts. Work 8 rows in garter stitch

Row 1 (RS): k4, *p4, k2, repeat from *, k4.
Row 2 and all even numbered rows: knit all knits and purl all purls.
Row 3: k4, *p3, k3, repeat from *, k4.
Row 5: k4, *p2, k4, repeat from *, k4.
Row 7: k4, p1, *k4, p2, repeat from *, end k4, p1, k4.
Row 9: k4, p1, *k3, p3, repeat from *, end k3, p2, k4.
Row 11: k4, p1, *k2, p4, repeat from *, end k2, p3, k4.

Repeat rows 1-12 another 3 times.

Work 8 rows in garter stitch. Bind off.

Finishing
Weave in ends, wash and block gently.

TREE HUNTING

by Chelsea Berkompas

This is a charming dishcloth with a 3-stitch garter border and a simple lace pattern reminiscent of a field of Christmas trees. Knit up a couple of these as gifts for loved ones or as a touch of holiday cheer to your own kitchen – can't you just feel the chilly air and smell the fresh pine as you meander through the tree farm searching for the perfect tree?

FINISHED MEASUREMENTS
8.5" square

YARN
Knit Picks Dishie (100% Cotton; 190 yards/100g): Jalapeno 25785; 1 ball.

NEEDLES
US 7 (4.5 mm) straight or circular needles, or size to obtain gauge

NOTIONS
Yarn Needle

GAUGE
18 sts and 24 rows = 4" over Lace Stitch Pattern.

Notes:

Lace Stitch Pattern (worked flat)
Row 1: (WS) and all other WS rows: K3, Purl until 3 sts remain, K3.
Row 2: K6, [K2tog, YO, K1, YO, SSK, K5] 2x, K2tog, YO, K1, YO, SSK, K6
Row 4: K5, [K2tog, (K1, YO) 2x, K1, SSK, K3] 2x, K2tog, (K1, YO) 2x, K1, SSK, K5
Row 6: K4, [K2tog, K2, YO, K1, YO, K2, SSK, K1] 3x, K3
Row 8: K3, K2tog, [K3, YO, K1, YO, K3, Sl 1, K2tog, PSSO] 2x, K3, YO, K1, YO, K3, SSK, K3
Row 10: K4, [YO, SSK, K5, K2tog, YO, K1] 3x, K3
Row 12: K4, [YO, K1, SSK, K3, K2tog, K1, YO, K1] 3x, K3
Row 14: K4, [YO, K2, SSK, K1, K2tog, K2, YO, K1] 3x, K3
Row 16: K4, [YO, K3, Sl1, K2tog, PSSO, K3, YO, K1] 3x, K3

DIRECTIONS
With US size 7 knitting needles and yarn, loosely CO 37 stitches.

Border
Knit 5 rows even.

Dishcloth Body
Next row is a WS row. Begin the Lace Stitch Pattern on row 1. Repeat Lace Stitch Pattern (rows 1-16) 3 times total.

Next row is a WS row: K3, Purl until 3 stitches remain, K3.

Border
K 5 rows even.

BO all stitches loosely.

Finishing
Weave in ends, wash and block if desired

GLACIAL SPA CLOTH

by Beth Major

This crocheted spa cloth in an icy blue is a perfect soothing complement for a spa day or just daily pampering.

FINISHED MEASUREMENTS
11" square, blocked

YARN
Knit Picks Shine Sport (60% Pima Cotton, 40% Modal; 110 yards/50g): Sky 23621; 1 ball.

HOOKS
US G/6 (4mm)

NOTIONS
Yarn Needle
Stitch Markers

GAUGE
8 sts and 4 rows = 2" in DC, lightly blocked

Notes:
FSC – Foundation Single Crochet
CH2, insert hook in 2nd CH from hook, pull up a loop, CH 1, yarn over, pull though both loops on hook (SC made) *insert hook through CH 1 and pull up a loop, CH 1, yarn over, pull through both loops on hook (SC made)* repeat from * to * until desired number is reached.

DIRECTIONS
Row 1: FSC 41.

Row 2: CH 1, turn, (SC, 2 DC, TR) in first st, sk next 3 sts, *(SC, 2 DC, TR) in next st, sk next 3 sts* repeat across row, SC in last st.

Row 3: CH 1, turn, (SC, 2 DC, TR) in first SC, sk next 3 SC, *(SC, 2 DC, TR) in next st, sk next 3 SC* repeat across row, SC in last st.

Repeat row 3 until cloth measures about 10 inches.

Finishing
Round 1: Ch 1, turn, SC in each st across, 3 SC in last SC of row, work 41 SC along edge, 3 SC in next corner, work SC in each st across, 3 Sc in next corner, work 41 SC along last edge, 3 SC in last corner, join last st to first st with a SL ST. CH 1 and fasten off.

Weave in ends and lightly block if desired

VADSTENA

by Allyson Dykhuizen

Vadstena Castle in Sweden took 75 years to build, but I promise this dishcloth won't take you nearly that long! Vadstena is surrounded by a moat, much like this dishcloth is surrounded by applied icord. TOTALLY the same thing.

FINISHED MEASUREMENTS
7.5" square measured side to side, 9.5" measured diagonally, 1.25" hanging loop.

YARN
Knit Picks CotLin (70% Tanguis Cotton, 30% Linen; 123 yards/50g);): Raindrop (MC) 25326, Conch (CC) 25776; 1 ball each.

NEEDLES
US 5 (3.75mm) 16" circular and 2 DPNs, or size to obtain gauge

NOTIONS
Yarn Needle
Small Crochet Hook

GAUGE
22 sts and 28 rows = 4" in Plaid Pattern, blocked.

Notes:
The body of the dishcloth is worked, then stitches are picked up around and an applied icord is worked before adding a little loop hanger to finish.

Completing Vertical Plaid Columns:
With CC held on WS and beginning at top of first purl column, insert crochet hook from RS into first st of purl column and pull up a loop of yarn from underneath. *Leaving loop on hook, insert hook from RS into next st of purl column and pull up a loop from underneath, pull this second loop through first loop, rep from * to last purl st, cut yarn and pull tail through last loop. Insert hook through last loop from WS and pull yarn tail to WS.

DIRECTIONS
With circular needles and MC CO 37 sts

Rows 1 and 3 (RS): With MC, k3, *p1, k4; rep from * to last 4 sts, p1, k3.

Rows 2 and 4 (WS): With MC, p3, *k1, p4; rep from * to last 4 sts, k1, p3. Cut MC after Row 4.

Rows 5: With CC work as for Row 1.

Row 6: With MC work as for Row 2.

Row 7: With MC work as for Row 1. Cut MC.

Row 8: With CC work as for Row 2.

Rows 9 and 10: With MC work as for Rows 1 and 2.

Work rows 1-10 5 times total, then rows 1-3 once more.

BO all Sts.

Complete Vertical Plaid Columns as described in Notes.

Finishing
Weave in ends, block to make a 7x7" square measured side to side, 9" diagonally across dishcloth.

Applied ICord
With circular needle and starting at your BO edge, pick up but do not knit 28 sts along each side of the square – 112 sts.

With CC, CO 2 sts on left needle. K3 – 2 CO sts and the first picked up stitch. Slide these stitches back to left hand needle. *K2, sl 1, k1, psso – 3 sts on right needle. Slip these stitches back to left hand needle. Rep from * until all picked up stitches are worked – 3 sts.

Swich to DPNs and work an icord for 2 ½". Cut yarn leaving a long tail and pull end through remaining stitches. Sew this end to the start of applied icord to attach, and put a little stitch at the top to join the bottom of your hanging loop. Weave in ends and block again to measurements.

SNOWBANK SPA CLOTH

by Alison Griffith

This luxurious spa cloth's surface mimicks the way snow drfts softly over the landscape, smoothing out the regular textures into gentle lumps and bumps. This washcloth is knit from the bottom up in a single piece, with a garter stitch border worked around the edge of the slipped stitch pattern.

FINISHED MEASUREMENTS
7" square

YARN
Knit Picks Comfy Sport (75% Pima Cotton, 25% Acrylic; 126 yards/50g): White 24794; 1 ball.

NEEDLES
US 6 (4mm) straight or circular needles, or size to obtain gauge

NOTIONS
Yarn Needle

GAUGE
28 sts and 40 rows = 4" in Texture Pattern, blocked.

DIRECTIONS
CO 36 sts and prepare to work back and forth.

K 3 rows (garter stitch).

K3 (M1, K3) across (47 sts).

Work Snowbank Chart, repeating pattern 10 times across each row

Work rows 1-8 7 times, then work rows 1-4 once more.

K3, (k2tog, k2) across (36 sts).

K 3 rows.

BO loosely.

Finishing
Weave in ends and block lightly.

Snowbank Chart

Legend

- ☐ **knit**
  RS: knit stitch
  WS: purl stitch

- • **purl**
  RS: purl stitch
  WS: knit stitch

- V **slip**
  RS: Slip stitch as if to purl, holding yarn in back
  WS: Slip stitch as if to purl, holding yarn in front

- ☐ **Pattern Repeat**

MEET THE DESIGNERS

Despite telling her mom years ago that she would never become a knitter, **Chelsea Berkompas** took up a pair of needles in 2009 and hasn't put them down since. She loves taking inspiration from the natural world around her and translating it into a one-of-a-kind design that is as simple and enjoyable to knit, as it is to wear. Keeping busy by day as a wife, mother and homemaker, Chelsea likes to spend her evenings curled up on the couch with a cup of coffee, knitting and sketching her never-ending design ideas. .
For pattern support, please contact chberkom@gmail.com

The Knit Picks Design Team
For pattern support, please contact customerservice@Knit Picks.com

Allyson Dykhuizen is a knitwear designer and knitting teacher from Michigan who lives in Chicago. Her patterns have been published in Interweave Knits, Knitscene, and knit.wear magazines, by Lion Brand Yarns, and included in the Knit Picks Independent Designer Program. She can be found on Ravelry at sweatshopoflove, self publishes and blogs on her website The Sweatshop of Love, and is the editor of Holla Knits.
For pattern support, please contact allyson@thesweatshopoflove.com

Joyce Fassbender is a biology lecturer in New York City. She recently got a puppy that she's training to be a good knitting dog, but not to knit because, sadly, it can't hold the needles. When not playing with the puppy, she's obsessing over shawls and lace.
For pattern support, please contact joycef2@gmail.com

Teresa Gregorio has been designing knitwear since 2007. Her love of fashion, history, art, knitting and making things happily collide on her blog, Canary Knits. For pattern support, please contact: canaryknitsdesigns@gmail.com

Allison Griffith is a lifelong knitter with years of experience designing patterns and teaching fiber arts. She is the creator and author of the blog On the Needles (www.ontheneedles.com) where she offers patterns, tutorials, and inspiration to hundreds of readers. When not knitting, Allison divides her time between working in her garden, watching too many Law & Order reruns, and playing with her dog.
For pattern support, please contact knittingontheneedles@gmail.com

Gillian Wynne Grimm lives in a little white cottage on a tree-lined street in Portland, Oregon where she knits, sews and generally enjoys making all manner of crafty and creative things.
Follow along with her adventures at Birchhollowcottage.com.
For pattern support, please contact info@birchhollowcottage.com

Kalurah Hudson's love of the Fiber Arts budded from an early life surrounded by art. But knitting and crocheting has just recently become this northwest native's newest love. She learned from a friend in late 2008 and now designs her own knit and crochet creations. This happy wife and mom of 3 dreams of some day living on an alpaca farm and starting up a fiber studio with built in coffee bistro.
For pattern support, please contact kalurah@whiletheyplay.com

Born and raised on eastern Long Island, NY, **Erica Jackofsky** grew up surrounded by the arts— performing (playing fiddle, flatfoot dancing, and singing) and traveling around the country with her family band, The Homegrown String Band. During her travels, Erica discovered knitting and crocheting and it wasn't long before the kid who fiddles to a different drummer was accumulating a yarn stash and designing her own projects. In early 2009 Erica established Fiddle Knits Designs and began to focus her energies on designing and creating original patterns inspired by music.
For pattern support, please contact Erica@FiddleKnits.com

Born in Sault Ste. Marie, Ontario, **Beth Major** learned to crochet and knit at a young age from her grandmother and while the needles confounded her, she really got hooked on crochet. Influenced by her upbringing in Northern Ontario, her designs tend to trend toward items for winter wear and home coziness. With a yarn stash that seems to breed in various closets and corners of her house, she often has at least 4 to 5 projects on the go at any one time and, when an idea sparks inspiration, will happily begin a new crochet project (or projects).
For pattern support, please contact crochetgypsy@gmail.com

Kendra Nitta's handknits designs have been featured in numerous books and magazines, and are available through Knit Picks and on Ravelry. She also sews and designs quilts. Follow along at www.missknitta.com and on Twitter at @missknitta..
For pattern support, please contact missknitta@gmail.com

Faith Schmidt designs under the name DistractedKnits for a very good reason. With nine children in the house, there's always something going on! This has led her to design patterns that are interesting to knit, but are also easy to memorize and "read", in case of one of those all-to-frequent interruptions. Faith can be found online at http://DistractedKnits.weebly.com and on Ravelry, Pinterest, Instagram and Twitter as DistractedKnits.
For pattern support, please contact DistractedKnits@hotmail.com

Crochet Abbreviations

beg	beginning	lp(s)	loop(s)	SL	slip
BLP	single or double crochet in back loop only	PM	place marker	sl st	slip stitch
		rem	remaining	st(s)	stitch(es)
BPDC	back post double crochet	rep	repeat	tr	treble crochet
ch(s)	chain(s)	RM	remove marker	TCH	top of turning chain made at start of previous row
ch-sp	chain space	rnd(s)	round(s)		
DC	double crochet	SC	single crochet	YO	yarn over
FSC	foundation single crochet	SC2tog	single crochet two together	* *	repeat directions given from * to *
FPDC	front post double crochet	shell	a group of stitches all worked in the same stitch		
HDC	half double crochet				

Knit Abbreviations

		LH	left hand	Rev St st	reverse stockinette stitch	sts	stitch(es)
BO	bind off	M	marker			TBL	through back loop
cn	cable needle	M1	make one stitch	RH	right hand	TFL	through front loop
CC	contrast color	M1L	make one left-leaning stitch	rnd(s)	round(s)	tog	together
CDD	Centered double dec			RS	right side	W&T	wrap & turn (see specific instructions in pattern)
CO	cast on	M1R	make one right-leaning stitch	Sk	skip		
cont	continue			Sk2p	sl 1, k2tog, pass slipped stitch over k2tog: 2 sts dec		
dec	decrease(es)	MC	main color			WE	work even
DPN(s)	double pointed needle(s)	P	purl			WS	wrong side
		P2tog	purl 2 sts together	SKP	sl, k, psso: 1 st dec	WYIB	with yarn in back
EOR	every other row	PM	place marker	SL	slip	WYIF	with yarn in front
inc	increase	PFB	purl into the front and back of stitch	SM	slip marker	YO	yarn over
K	knit			SSK	sl, sl, k these 2 sts tog		
K2tog	knit two sts together	PSSO	pass slipped stitch over	SSP	sl, sl, p these 2 sts tog tbl		
KFB	knit into the front and back of stitch	PU	pick up	SSSK	sl, sl, sl, k these 3 sts tog		
K-wise	knitwise	P-wise	purlwise				
		rep	repeat	St st	stockinette stitch		

Knit Picks yarn is both luxe and affordable—a seeming contradiction trounced! But it's not just about the pretty colors; we also care deeply about fiber quality and fair labor practices, leaving you with a gorgeously reliable product you'll turn to time and time again.

THIS COLLECTION FEATURES

Dishie
Worsted Weight
100% Cotton

Shine Worsted
Worsted Weight
60% Pima Cotton, 40% Modal

Shine Sport
Sport Weight
60% Pima Cotton, 40% Modal

Comfy Worsted
Worsted Weight
75% Pima Cotton, 25% Acrylic

Comfy Sport
Sport Weight
75% Pima Cotton, 25% Acrylic

Simply Cotton Worsted
Worsted Weight
100% Organic Cotton

CotLin
DK Weight
70% Tanguis Cotton, 30% Linen

View these beautiful yarns and more at www.KnitPicks.com